A dream of centuries has come true with the taming of the rapids in the great St. Lawrence River and the construction of locks and dams for navigation and for electric power. *St. Lawrence Seaway* is the exciting story of men and machines and the co-operation of two nations in building the seaway.

ST. LAWRENCE SEAWAY

ST. LAWRENCE

Eisenhower Lock

Long Sault Dam

Snell Lock

Drawings by Lorence F. Bjorklund

Illustrated with Photographs of the Seaway

SEAWAY

CLARA INGRAM JUDSON

Moses-Saunders Powerhouse

Follett Publishing Company

Chicago

The Library of Congress has catalogued this book as follows:

Judson, Clara (Ingram) 1879–
    St. Lawrence Seaway. Illustrated with photos of the seaway.
Maps and drawings by Lorence F. Bjorklund. Chicago,
Follett Pub. Co. [1959]

    160 p. illus. 24 cm.

1. St. Lawrence Seaway.

HD1694.A254J8   627.12   59–8989 ‡

    Library of Congress

*The author and publisher wish to express their appreciation to the following
for the photographs and some of the maps used in* St. Lawrence Seaway: *Allis Chalmers,
p. 140; Chicago Aerial Industries, Inc. p. 150; Inland Steel Company, p. 144; Montreal
Tourist and Convention Bureau, p. 159; Mississippi Valley Barge Line Company, p. 149;
Ontario Hydro, p. 108, 113, 114, 116, 135; Power Authority of the State of New York,
p. 111, 115, 117, 124, 131, 134, 155 (top), also title page; St. Lawrence Municipal Bureau,
Montreal, p. 154 (top); St. Lawrence Seaway Authority, p. 99, 128, 129, 139 (top), 154
(bottom); U. S. Army Corps of Engineers, kodachrome for cover, p. 139 (bottom), p. 155
(bottom); United States Steel Company, p. 94; and the map department of Follett Publishing
Company for maps on pages 8, 9, 10, 120, 121.*

Author's Foreword

The St. Lawrence Seaway and power project is one of the technical wonders of our time, but that fact alone would not have prompted me to write this book. Far more remarkable than powerhouse, great dams, and long deep locks is the fact that, in this particular period of world tensions and fears, two nations have joined in planning, constructing, paying for, and using facilities for navigation and for power on their unfortified frontiers. Such faith, such co-operation, is new in world history and is immeasurably heartening. How did it come about?

For full understanding one must go back—far back to the time when the Great Lakes and their river to the sea were formed, to the people who came to live by the waters, their habits, their wars, their dreams. This study has been long and fascinating; the final story is documented history. For vividness I have chosen to present some incidents in the form of dramatic scenes rather than the more usual straight narration. Such scenes fall into two sorts, historical and contemporary. The historical incidents are gleaned from old reports, letters, and documents available in libraries and archives. When such authentic sources report that a certain man "said," I allow that man to say his words instead of imposing upon him the less vivid third person form. For instance, throughout the seventeenth century the annual Jesuit Relations (reports) are rich in such quotable material, and there are annual reports to French kings, letters, and other documents. Contemporary conversations are those I heard or shared and wrote down immediately while traveling along the seaway during its construction.

One of my major problems has been what to include here about Sault Ste. Marie. It is not a part of the actual St. Lawrence Seaway, but it is a vital link in the Great Lakes–St. Lawrence waterway. I have had to remind myself often that the 500-year history of that fabulous mile has already been published in my book, *The Mighty Soo* (Follett, 1955) and is available to anyone who wishes to know more about that gateway to the north.

I am deeply indebted to many agencies and many people for help in gathering facts and pictures for this book. Among these are three

United States agencies: the St. Lawrence Seaway Development Corporation, the Power Authority of the State of New York, and the U. S. Army, Corps of Engineers, North Central Division—with special gratitude to the engineers for reading my galley proof; three Canadian agencies: the St. Lawrence Seaway Authority, the Hydro Electric Commission of Ontario, and the Canadian Consulate General, Chicago. Among other helpful agencies have been Deering Library, Northwestern University, Newberry Library, the Chicago Regional Port District, and the Lake Carriers Association.

In addition to studying the vast amount of material provided from these sources, I have studied magazines, newspapers, brochures, and more than a hundred books, and have interviewed scores of informed persons in an effort to get the whole story.

Among individuals who were especially helpful are Mr. Donald LaChance of Evanston, who loaned me rare, old books; Miss Jean Gogo, at the Cornwall Public Library in Canada, who located for me material about old canals; Miss Florence Davison, at the Evanston Public Library, who helped me in historical research, and Miss Louise Borchelt, who kept me informed about new publications and arranged private showings of new films on the seaway. In August of 1957, when thousands of men were working along the seaway, my brother, Dwight Ingram, and his son, Tom, drove me along the entire seaway area. We stopped several days at the busiest places; we drove on the dry and dusty bottom of the drained Long Sault rapids, dodging rocks, slithering in sand —a dramatic experience, for each of us had taken the voyage down those dangerous waters in the *Rapids Prince*, and now the great rocks are hidden forever in the depths of the new Lake St. Lawrence. We ended our journey by driving across the Jacques Cartier Bridge on a day when great changes were being made and the approaches swarmed with men and machines.

All this and much more has gone into the writing of *St. Lawrence Seaway*. It is my hope that some of the inspiration of seeing the labor and faith of two co-operating nations will reach out through picture and story and will move the reader to new hope for world peace.

C.I.J.

Evanston, Illinois
March 1, 1959

ST. LAWRENCE **SEAWAY**

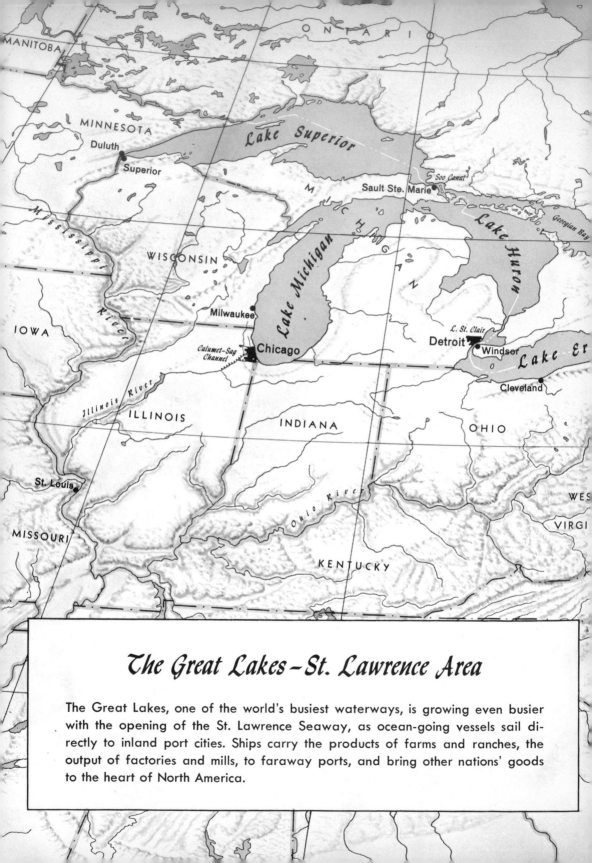

The Great Lakes–St. Lawrence Area

The Great Lakes, one of the world's busiest waterways, is growing even busier with the opening of the St. Lawrence Seaway, as ocean-going vessels sail directly to inland port cities. Ships carry the products of farms and ranches, the output of factories and mills, to faraway ports, and bring other nations' goods to the heart of North America.

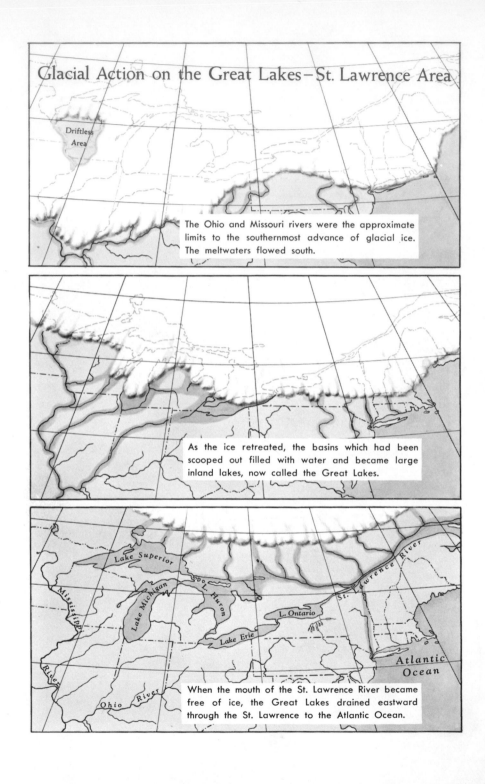

Glacial Action on the Great Lakes – St. Lawrence Area

Driftless Area

The Ohio and Missouri rivers were the approximate limits to the southernmost advance of glacial ice. The meltwaters flowed south.

As the ice retreated, the basins which had been scooped out filled with water and became large inland lakes, now called the Great Lakes.

Lake Superior

Lake Michigan

L. Huron

Mississippi

L. Ontario

St. Lawrence River

Lake Erie

Atlantic Ocean

Ohio River

When the mouth of the St. Lawrence River became free of ice, the Great Lakes drained eastward through the St. Lawrence to the Atlantic Ocean.

CHAPTER I

The Beginning

ICE began the making of the Great Lakes–St. Lawrence waterway. Great glaciers—shoving, grinding—hollowed out the five huge basins that, together, hold the greatest body of fresh water on the earth. Imagine trying to make such excavations, even with the machines of today! The draglines and derricks, the fifteen-ton scoops and huge trucks, would be helpless in excavating the Lake Superior basin, 400 miles long and 1300 feet deep. And there are four more basins, all except Lake Erie very deep. Where would the spoil bank be? What could be done with all the earth and stone scooped out of the Lake Superior basin alone? The glaciers, of course, had no problem; unhurriedly the rivers of ice spread material over half a continent.

As the climate grew warmer, the ice melted, filling the present Great Lakes and much of the country around them, and flowing away to the south. Ages later, when the inland sea receded, the Mississippi no longer drained the Great Lakes Basin; now it drains northeastward to the Atlantic. On its 2342-mile journey to the sea, the water falls 600 feet; sometimes in short drops, once—at Niagara —in one mighty plunge, falling 165 feet with a roar that can be heard for miles.

The country around the lakes is rich in minerals, on the earth's surface and hidden beneath it—iron and copper, gold and silver, uranium, and probably other deposits of ore yet to be discovered. Forests of hardwoods, birch, and pine grew after the ice had gone. Animals wearing soft furs thrived in the wilderness along the lakes and rivers. These riches suggest commerce; water was there for cheap transport. But commerce is the business of men, and as yet there were no men by the lakes, though men were coming....

They were coming from three directions, north, south, and east. The day when men would think of the long waterway as a highway to the sea was still distant, but with the arrival of men, the possibility drew nearer.

The first men to reach the Great Lakes came from the north. They had set out from Asia, perhaps by way of the Aleutian Islands, in one of the greatest, most mysterious migrations in history. Slowly they traveled south and east, stopping sometimes for a year, sometimes for a generation or two. Some of them spread out along the lakes and the great river and came to be called Algonquins. They made the first boats on the lakes, grace-ful birchbark canoes, useful in fishing and in travel.

A second mighty migration brought people from the south.

While they traveled, the old women told stories to the chil-dren. They always ended the same way:

"Remember that you come from a land that is always warm.

... Remember that there the trees had leaves like swords," the old women told the children as they moved north. Perhaps the trees were tropical palms and the people Aztecs. No one really knows, but the story was told from generation to generation and became a legend.

They were a strange people, interested in politics and government more than in the simple arts of living. Each village where they paused a while had a large Long House for a meeting place for warriors and chiefs and carelessly built huts as shelters for the people. They were not skillful with their hands; their boats were hollowed-out logs, awkward and unseaworthy on the lakes.

The people from the south coveted the swift birchbark canoes and thick warm furs of the Algonquins; what they coveted, they took by force. Early contacts were few, because the lakes were wide and the boats small; but as both peoples came to the river, the fighting was vicious. The men from the south were known as Iroquois, the Enemy. Iroquois, the Destroyers. The name became a word of terror.

Long afterward, the third migration began, the movement of Europeans toward the Western Hemisphere. The first Europeans to cross the Atlantic seem to have been Norse adventurers who, in their incredibly small boats, sailed to Greenland and on down the coast of North America.

A book written in a Genoese prison in the thirteenth century was an indirect cause of westward exploration. *The Book of Marco Polo* told of the author's adventures in the rich Mongol Empire in the Far East. It inspired daring men who longed for adventure and kings and courtiers who wanted the gold and jewels and other wealth of the Orient. But the book also told of the dangers of desert travel—the heat, thirst, and wild tribes encountered. Were silks and gold and jewels worth the risk?

Almost two centuries later, *The Book of Marco Polo* was printed for the first time on the newly invented printing press. Again men who read it had their dreams and ambitions stirred. The Turks had cut off most of the old trade routes to the Orient, but surely there were other ways of getting to the riches of China, or Cathay, as they called it.

Portuguese sailors had long been sailing south along the coast of Africa, searching for a sea route to the Indies. An Italian, Christopher Columbus, had a new idea: since the earth was round, why couldn't one sail *west* and reach the Orient?

Columbus's success was greater than he ever dreamed; but he did not find a passage to the Far East. Nor did any of the explorers who followed him. And until a third of the sixteenth century had passed, none of them came to the wide river that poured water from the five Great Lakes into the sea.

During this same period, common folk of Europe, living along the Atlantic shore, sailed farther and farther west, fishing for cod. They seem to have done some trading in furs with Indians; common people in Europe had North American furs long before they were fashionable in court circles. But these fishermen did not explore farther west, nor did they have any idea of the great waterway that led into the heart of the continent.

Then a Frenchman, Jacques Cartier, persuaded his king, Francis I, that he could find a northwest passage through the land barrier and bring the riches of the East to France. Cartier had made friends at court who helped him to win the king's support. Soon he was sailing west with two ships and sixty men, in search of a northwest passage to China. He made no important discoveries on the first trip, but he did bring back fine furs and two Indians, thought to be sons of a chief. The furs delighted the king; the Indians were a novelty at court and also a help to Cartier in learning something of Indian languages and customs.

The next year, Cartier sailed west again. During this second voyage, on August 10th, 1535, he discovered the hundred-mile-wide gulf that he named St. Lawrence, because the day was St. Lawrence' Day. Cartier sailed on up the river that he gave the same name until he came to a narrow stretch and a great rock on the northern shore. He called the place Kebec, an Algonquian word meaning the Narrows, and later changed the spelling to Quebec. It was at this time that he first heard the word Kanata—or was it Canada? He was not sure. The Indians seemed to use the word to mean a village.

The plan had been to have the two young Indians guide Cartier on up the river, looking for the northwest passage, but they refused. They seemed to be afraid of some other tribe; this was Cartier's first knowledge of the long warfare along the river. The leader and a few men went on in a small boat, without guides. They found the island with a mountain that the Indians had spoken of, and drew up to shore amidst a crowd of curious strangers, seemingly of another tribe.

"What name do you give this place?" Cartier asked them as he stepped ashore.

"Hochelaga," one said. They seemed surprised to hear Indian words.

"*Hochelaga!*" Cartier fairly spat out the harsh word. "That is no name for this beautiful place. I shall call it Mount Royal for my king." And so he did, in his report.

As they talked, Cartier kept hearing the roar of waters off to the south. He had his men push away from the shore and row in that direction. They soon came to the foot of a rapids where water dashed high and currents swirled.

"La Sault!" Cartier cried, astonished at the sight. He used the French word for falls or rapids. The roar was deafening as the sailors tried in vain to push up against the mighty current.

"If this is the way to China, the journey will be difficult," Cartier said, much puzzled. His handsome coat was soaked; he and his men were weary. Cartier named the place Sault La Chine

—the rapids of China—and then returned to the island.

The Indians were still on the shore and took the strangers up the mountain to see their village—a Long House surrounded by small huts on the same level place where, long afterward, St. James Cathedral was built. Then Cartier went back to Quebec.

The Frenchmen stayed through the long, cold winter, but they could do little exploring; cold and illness depleted the crew. And the winter changed Cartier. He ceased to value fame and wealth. He

wanted to get fresh supplies and then return and convert these strange wild Indians to Christianity.

But in France, the following summer, his report was scorned. Francis I was not interested in missionary work; Cartier was accounted a failure. He had discovered a great waterway as far inland as the first rapids, but no one thought that was important.

Cartier seemed to be forgotten in his own time, but centuries later, his name was given to a handsome bridge across the St. Lawrence at Montreal. The northern approach to the bridge is near the place where Cartier landed, on that October day in 1535. Today the bridge marks the eastern end of the St. Lawrence Seaway. Its lofty span, crowded with traffic, stands as a welcome or farewell to ships of all nations and proclaims that Jacques Cartier and his courage and imagination are remembered.

*   *   *   *   *   *

By the beginning of the seventeenth century, the long religious wars in France ended. Henry of Navarre had become a Catholic and was king of France; a new era seemed to be dawning. Men turned their thoughts from war to everyday matters, and even to the New World. The discoverer of the northwest passage would gain fame; but even without that, a voyage to the New World would be rewarding. There were souls to save and furs to take back to France.

"Furs might pay for salvation," someone said, and the phrase was repeated to Francis Pontgravé, a merchant of St. Malo.

Pontgravé had done some trading in American furs; he knew their possibilities as a source of wealth.

"We could take settlers over, too," he said. "That would please the king." But this plan required ships and a navigator.

Samuel de Champlain was recommended; he was both a navigator and a cartographer, and he had won the king's favor as a soldier. So it came about that in 1603, sixty-nine years after Cartier's first voyage, a new expedition set out across the sea for a region hopefully called New France.

At Quebec Pontgravé stayed to develop his trading, and Champlain went on up the river. He found the beautiful island and the mountain as Cartier had reported, but no village. He found the Sault La Chine and tried to ascend the rapids. As the crew of the long boat toiled, Champlain noticed two Indians lurking on the bank, watching. He stepped ashore and, in the few Indian words he knew, asked them about the river.

"They seem to tell of small lakes above, and more rapids," he translated to his men. "A long rapids, more river, and a big lake with Niagara above—now, what could that mean?" The Indians, sensing that he did not understand, roared frighteningly and then added, "and more lakes."

"Probably they make fun of me," Champlain decided. "Pontgravé says some Indians like to tease. Surely no place in the world has so many connected lakes and rivers!"

This first idea of the length of the waterway seemed so incredible that Champlain dismissed it from his mind. He did go on up the Sault La Chine, across two pretty lakes, and to the foot of a long rapids—about where the new powerhouse stands now. He stood in the prow of the boat while his men tried to hold it steady, and studied the view upstream.

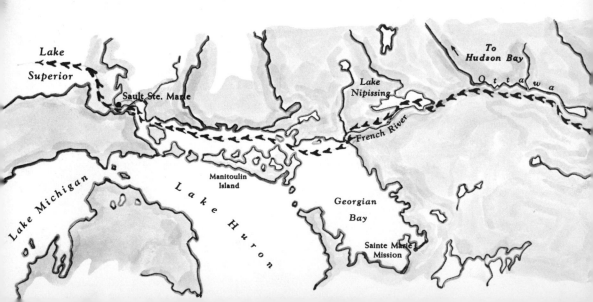

"A long sault," he said, discouraged. Champlain had no time
for a longer journey, so he turned back and spent some weeks
exploring downriver. He found the lake that bears his name and
mapped that whole region. In the meantime, Pontgravé had established several trading posts for furs.

In the next few years the two leaders returned often to the
New World. On his voyage in 1608, Champlain brought with him a
youth named Etienne Brulé, whom he left to live with the Hurons,
to learn Indian ways and language. It is now believed that Brulé
was the first European to see all five of the Great Lakes, the easterly
two while on a mission for Champlain, the others while exploring
with a friend.

Warring Indians and travel difficulties, however, made traders
continue to use the so-called northern route along the Ottawa River.
Champlain had built a trading post on the north shore of the St.
Lawrence between the mouth of the Ottawa and the village of

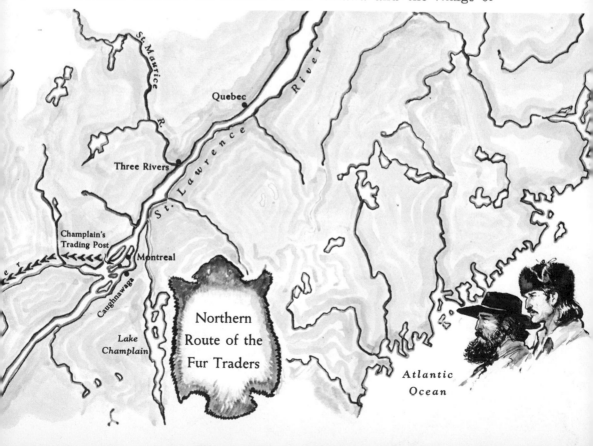

Northern
Route of the
Fur Traders

Montreal. The sturdy building was made of heavy timbers; its chimney was twenty-eight and a half feet high and nine feet wide at the base—a marvel for the time and place. Behind the wide fireplace were ovens for roasting and baking.

This trading post was famous for years, and its chimney stood for two hundred years after the building fell to ruins. The site is near the north end of the Honoré Mercier Bridge (1935), one of the important bridges along the seaway. The south end of the bridge is near Caughnawaga, the old Iroquois village where Indians watched for traders to come to the post.

For many years Champlain labored for New France; he is called "the Father of Canada," an honor he earned through long and faithful service to the people along the St. Lawrence River. His death in 1635 came at a time when the New World was changing fast. The English had settlements on the James River and in Massachusetts and Maryland, the Dutch on Manhattan Island and up the Hudson. The aims of these later arrivals differed from those of the French. The English and Dutch wanted to clear the wilderness and make farms; the French needed the wilderness and the Indians for their profitable fur trade.

In the meantime, the English and Dutch wanted furs too, but the southern furs which the Iroquois offered were not thick and beautiful like the northern furs so popular in Europe. So the Iroquois began raiding across the waterway—slyly at first, then boldly. In this way the English and Dutch, quite unwittingly, added to the long warfare across the river and lakes.

None of the new North Americans seem to have thought of the waterway as a whole and its possibilities as a highway. The idea of a connected, usable waterway was first conceived by two men who came to the New World from France a generation after Champlain.

CHAPTER 2

Men and a Dream

THE year 1666 was important in the story of the Great Lakes–St. Lawrence waterway, for in that year two men with widely different natures and ambitions arrived in New France. Both were to discover a connection between the Great Lakes and Mississippi basins and to realize what such a link might mean to North America. These men were Father Marquette, a priest, and Robert Cavelier, a businessman, later called La Salle.

Father Marquette had been sent from France to bring fresh inspiration to the missions of the Roman Catholic Church. Under Champlain's influence, the work of the church had prospered until the late 1640's. Jesuits, following the early Recollect priests, had gone far into the wilderness; they had established churches and taught the Indians, and they had built a retreat on the Wye River near the present city of Midland, Ontario. They called the place Sainte Marie.

But in the decade beginning in 1640, the Iroquois constantly raided the area between Lake Huron and Lake Erie to get northern furs. By 1650 they had completely destroyed many missions and the Sainte Marie retreat. After this, the work of the church faltered. Fifteen years passed before Father Allouez was sent out, not to Lake Huron, but beyond, to Lake Superior. He opened a mission among the Cree Indians at La Pointe, near the site of the present city of Ashland. A few Indians had brought furs from this distant place, but Father Allouez' mission was the first real connection between the Lake Superior region and New France.

Father Marquette, a more dynamic man than Father Allouez, was sent to this La Pointe mission. On his way he stopped at the rapids, built a church, and gave the place its name, Sault Ste. Marie.

The two priests occasionally talked of a great river that Father Allouez had heard was not far away.

"Some think it flows to a western sea," he said.

"A great river!" Marquette's imagination flared. "Men have been searching for an outlet to the western sea. There are souls to be saved there as well as here."

But soon an order came to leave La Pointe to the Indians. Father Allouez was recalled, and Father Marquette was told to open a new mission at the head of Lake Michigan. He chose a site and called the new mission St. Ignace. It was a lonely place, off the known route by way of the Ottawa River, Georgian Bay, and Sault Ste. Marie.

In the meantime, disturbing news had come to the French king. Pierre Radisson of Three Rivers, on the St. Lawrence, had gone to Hudson Bay and found wonderful furs which he offered to the king. But neither the king nor his nobles were interested. So

the ambitious Radisson went to England, where the Hudson's
Bay Company was formed to import furs.

The news angered the French king and hurt both his pride and
his pocketbook. His answer was to send over Governor Talon with
orders to make clear that all of North America belonged to France.
The first task was to curb the Iroquois. French troops were sent out;
they defeated the Iroquois and burned their villages. Later a notable
ceremony was arranged for the Indians far in the wilderness; its
purpose was to convince them that they must take their furs to the
French on the St. Lawrence, not to the English at Hudson Bay.
Talon chose St. Lusson to represent him in this important task.

St. Lusson had a fine sense of the dramatic. He sent out messengers who gathered fourteen tribes of Indians at Sault Ste. Marie
in June of 1671. St. Lusson and his party arrived in state; the
hundreds of assembled Indians were much impressed. On the appointed day, St. Lusson, in brilliant court dress and supported by
priests whose black robes made him the more conspicuous, walked
to the bank by the rapids. There he planted the cross and the flag
of France, white with golden fleur-de-lis, and proclaimed that the
North American continent belonged to France. Then he waited
while a translator gave his news to the Indians. Now the word
would spread through the wilderness, and furs would be brought
to river ports.

All this brought attention to the Lake Superior region. For the
first time, people in Europe as well as along the St. Lawrence began
to realize that a great waterway lay off to the north. As a result,
on a cold winter day in 1672, a canoe drew up on the beach at St.
Ignace and a man walked toward the mission cabin.

"I am Louis Joliet," he said to Father Marquette, who came
to meet him. "Perhaps you remember me. I saw you at Sault Ste.
Marie."

"Of course I remember you, my son. Welcome!" As Marquette

raised his hands in a blessing, he thought to himself, a visitor! An answer to my prayers! The work of this Canadian-born explorer was well known to Marquette.

"I have new orders from your superiors," Joliet explained. "You are to come with me and find the Mississippi, the great River of the West."

The winter passed quickly while the two men made plans and gathered information from the Indians. In the spring they set out with five others in two canoes. The explorers were ill provided with supplies but had plenty of faith and courage.

They paddled to Green Bay and up the Fox River, and went by portage to the Wisconsin River—a route the Indians knew. To their delight, the Wisconsin flowed into a stately river guarded by high bluffs—surely the River of the West. But as they paddled downstream, Joliet grew anxious. "We seem to go steadily south," he said, "not toward a western sea but toward the Spaniards!"

Marquette agreed that it would not do to fall into the hands of the Spaniards.

So, after passing the mouth of the Missouri, the explorers turned back and went up the Illinois River. Father Marquette built a little church near where Peoria now is and worked with the friendly Indians there. By this time, the fiercer Iroquois had migrated to the east. Joliet explored farther. He found a short, easy portage to the Chicago River through a natural depression, a sag, in the remarkably low watershed between the Great Lakes and the Mississippi basins. He wrote a report and drew careful maps. Then it was decided that he should go to Quebec with his news of the great river and of the easy connecting link with the lakes. Father Marquette would return to St. Ignace later. In their joy of discovery, the two explorers thought of men in Quebec as eagerly awaiting their report.

Alas for their dreams! On the journey Joliet's canoe overturned, and his papers were lost. He nearly drowned trying to retrieve them. He made new maps and reports when he reached Quebec, but the men there would not believe him; they accused him of drawing from imagination, not memory. Nor was he believed in Paris, where his papers were sent. Joliet's permission to explore was withdrawn. Marquette died in loneliness two years later. Their vision of a simple connection between two vast water systems appeared to be forgotten.

The second traveler who came to New France in that year of 1666 was La Salle, a practical young man of twenty-three, the son of a merchant. When asked why he came, he answered frankly, "To join my brother and to make a fortune." He brought with him excellent letters of introduction and a grant of land on the river.

The land was well situated on the north shore of the St. Lawrence River, at the foot of Frazier's Hill, opposite the Lachine Rapids. Montreal was downstream a few miles, and the village of Lachine was two miles west. Champlain's trading post nearby had been enlarged. La Salle built his home near it, an unusual cabin designed with two large rooms, each with an outside door and windows. His land stretched far back; he could farm or raise livestock, and his good location by the river would attract fur traders. The Iroquois had been quiet for some time; their village, Caughnawaga, across the river, was thought to be deserted.

La Salle became skillful in dealing with Indians. Some of them visited in his home; they told him of a great river to the west that flowed into the sea. His mind became filled with new ideas for expanding the fur trade and exploring the unknown west.

The roar of the beautiful Lachine Rapids distracted La Salle. Whence came all the rushing water? He knew where it went— down to the sea. But westward some mighty force must send it dashing over those great rocks. La Salle began spending a good deal of time away from home, traveling in the wilderness. Exploring came to mean more to him than making money at a trading post.

Two events encouraged La Salle's new ambitions. Louis Joliet arrived with his maps and reports; La Salle was fascinated, perhaps the only man who believed Joliet. And a new governor, Count Frontenac, came out, with orders to find more wealth for the royal treasury. Where was it to be found but in the west? Frontenac had heard about La Salle and his explorations and invited him to join him in his enterprises.

In 1673, Frontenac planned a trip up the St. Lawrence River. This first official French expedition up the river from Montreal was an impressive one. In all, four hundred men, a hundred and fifty canoes, two flatboats with supplies, and a train of small boats called barques set out, cheered by crowds along the shore.

The formal procession ended at the rapids, where men began to pull and struggle against the current. The flotilla worried its way up the rapids, crossed two peaceful lakes, and came to the Long Sault, where the struggle was repeated, for thirty miles instead of eight.

As the expedition passed through the undemanding Thousand Islands section, someone noticed Indians, lurking, watching. So when a landing was made near where Kingston is now, Frontenac sent messengers to invite the Indians to a conference. Meanwhile, La Salle was given the task of building a fort. He inspired his men with enthusiasm, and they worked quickly. When the Indians arrived, a good defense was ready. The governor's stern manner— and the fort —impressed the Indians. They agreed upon peace.

Frontenac now felt that success was assured. He ordered La Salle to build two boats for transport of supplies between the mouth of the Niagara River and the fort at Kingston. These were the first sailing ships on any of the five lakes. But their use was limited; they could not climb the falls of Niagara, nor would La Salle risk taking them through the St. Lawrence rapids.

In the meantime, the governor had to return to his duties in Quebec. He left La Salle, who agreed to explore beyond Lake Ontario. He found Niagara Falls, saw the great escarpment and Lake Erie.

"I can build a boat on this lake," he decided. "Men could carry material up that escarpment to a river I saw."

So the *Griffin* was built on the Niagara River not far from Lake Erie. It carried five guns and was named in honor of Frontenac, who had griffins on his coat of arms. La Salle intended to use the

Griffin to transport furs and supplies between Niagara and a trading post on Lake Michigan. Frontenac trusted La Salle; he gave him the responsibility of establishing posts and developing trade.

La Salle planned with care. He sent two bateaux on ahead, one to St. Ignace, one to what is now called Washington Island. In the summer of 1679, the *Griffin* was outfitted and loaded and pulled around into Lake Erie. In twenty days, the *Griffin* had traveled through the St. Clair River and up Lake Huron to St. Ignace, but the advance guard was not there. La Salle left word and went on down Lake Michigan to Washington Island.

Here his men had fine furs awaiting the ship. The *Griffin* was loaded and sent back to the Niagara River while La Salle and the others went on down Lake Michigan to the mouth of the St. Joseph River.

The St. Ignace men did not come. The *Griffin* did not return. La Salle never saw that ship again. Its fate is the first of many mysterious disappearances of ships upon the Great Lakes.

To keep up the health and morale of his men, La Salle had them build a fort at St. Joseph—the first fort on Lake Michigan. When the St. Ignace group finally came, La Salle decided to move on at once and find the Illinois region of Joliet's report. Because of lake storms, he went by the St. Joseph River to the Kankakee and then to the Des Plaines and the Illinois—a new water route with only one easy portage. On that portage, La Salle and his men saw herds of buffalo; they marveled at the strange humpbacked animals.

In midwinter cold, they arrived at Starved Rock, where they could find shelter in one of Marquette's churches. Soon they went on to Lake Peoria. La Salle had planned to build a flatboat there to carry supplies down the Mississippi River.

A curious evil fate seemed to descend upon La Salle after the loss of the *Griffin*. His shipbuilders deserted, taking needed supplies. He had men build a fort, the first in the Mississippi valley, but they could not build the boat without ropes, canvas, tools. There was only one place to get such supplies, only one man with authority to ask for them, only one way to make the journey. La Salle set out at once, in winter, to walk to Montreal.

He walked around the tip of Lake Michigan, on the way discovering the southern sag, a second depression in the watershed which is now known as the Calumet Sag or Cal-Sag. He was impressed by the easy portage between the Mississippi system and the Great Lakes.

La Salle left no detailed record of that remarkable journey, but he got to Montreal in about two months. There he had difficulties with his supplies; it was nearly two years before he returned to the Illinois country by bateau. The flatboat was built, and the journey down the Mississippi was begun.

La Salle and his party were much pleased by the size of the river, the fertile soil, and the great quantities of game. They encountered Indians on the way, but had no serious problems. They arrived at the Gulf of Mexico on April 9, 1682.

The chronicler of that expedition recorded: "Advancing on, we discovered the open sea . . . on the ninth of April, with all possible solemnity, we performed the ceremony of planting the cross and raising the arms of France. . . . the Sieur de la Salle, in the name of His Majesty, took possession of that river, of all rivers that enter it and of all the country watered by them."

La Salle returned to Canada, going by way of the north sag, Chicago River to Lake Michigan. Then he went to France, where he was honored and given permission to return to the Gulf of Mexico and establish a French colony and forts, in order to keep this part of the country for France. In this he was unsuccessful, and he was killed on the expedition; but he had proved that men could go by water through the heart of the continent almost all the way from the St. Lawrence to the Gulf of Mexico.

La Salle's
Routes

————— 1679

················ 1682

Marquette
and
Joliet's Route

CHAPTER 3

The First Canal

THE later years of the 1600's brought
difficult times along the St. Lawrence River. La Salle and Marquette were dead; Joliet was discredited. No one had a thought for
travel or trade west—there were too many troubles at home.

Governor Frontenac's recall for reasons of court politics was a
blow to New France; he had had just the right mixture of sternness
and showmanship to keep the Iroquois in order. The new governor
did not understand Indians and would not take advice from men
with experience. All three nations—the Dutch, the English, and
the French—were guilty of giving the Indians firearms, ammuni-
tion, and alcohol—rum or brandy. Indians were not accustomed
to drinking, and alcohol inflamed the harsh side of their natures
and made them even more bold and dangerous than before.

They crossed the river and killed traders; they raided peaceful settlements; their attacks were so terrifying that for three years not a single bateau brought fur to port towns.

Farmers suffered, too. For decades, settlers had chosen to live by the river which was their highway. Farms stretched back, as La Salle's had. Now people hardly dared plant their fields. Instead of, "God calls to worship," the ringing of a church bell often meant, "Iroquois are coming! Beware!" Men, women, and children dropped tools and ran for the nearest stockade, often too late to save their lives.

During this time one of the most stirring incidents in Canadian history took place near Montreal. Word came that the Iroquois were up by the Ottawa River and were coming down to destroy Montreal. People panicked, as well they might; the town was not fortified. Then sixteen young men volunteered to go up the Ottawa, take a position in a discarded stockade—and save Montreal. People stared at each other, white-faced.

"Sixteen? How could sixteen men save a city?"

"We can do our best," the young men said. They went up the Ottawa. They repaired the stockade, and waited. At dawn of the third day came the Iroquois war whoops. The young men took their stand and kept up steady fire until the Iroquois dead piled up so high that other braves could climb over the dead and into the stockade.

It took only minutes to kill the sixteen defenders. Then the Iroquois looked for the rest of the force—sixteen dead men were all they found. But if sixteen Montrealers could kill more than five hundred trained warriors, what might Montreal hold for attackers? The Indians turned back, slipped away without even burying their dead. Montreal was saved.

Some time later, Iroquois did venture across and wipe out the village of Lachine. Urgent letters were sent to the king.

"Send us Frontenac!"

The very sight of the count, now a vigorous man of seventy, brought comfort to the French; and word of his arrival was bad news to the Indians. Frontenac at once began plans for a great conclave to end the Indian wars. The plans might take years, for he meant the meeting to be successful.

Now that Frontenac had come, people resumed the usual pattern of living. Fields were planted; trade began again. But some people could not forget that raid upon Lachine, and there was talk about the need for a protected waterway. The Little St. Pierre River was near the north edge of the rapids; now, if it could be lengthened and connected with other waters . . . The Sulpician priests seem to have had a ditch or a kind of canal dug to connect

the little river with a branch of the Ottawa River to the east, nearer
Montreal. Fur traders extended it further, connecting the Little
St. Pierre with the mouth of the Ottawa. All together, the waterway
was some eight or ten miles long, eighteen inches deep, and five
feet wide. There were small wooden gates at both ends. Simple as
this waterway was, it allowed bateaux to be dragged out of sight
of the Indians lurking near Caughnawaga, and without the time
and labor needed for travel on the rapids. This first canal to bypass rapids on the St. Lawrence opened in 1700.

The beloved Frontenac did not live to see this canal or to take
part in the conclave he had planned. He died in 1698. Today in
Canada a traveler often sees the name "Frontenac"; the wise governor is justly honored for the work he did in the New World.

His successor, Governor Callières, wisely accepted Frontenac's
plans and held the conclave as the late governor had intended. It
took place in Montreal in the summer of 1701, and more than
fifteen hundred Algonquins and Iroquois attended.

It would be difficult to plan a more spectacular convention.
That rather small level area, part way up the mountain, where
Cartier had visited the Long House and the village, was the site
chosen. High above, the mountain was dark with great trees. To
the west was the Ottawa River, with its several outlets. In the east,
the great St. Lawrence River flowed quietly, and far to the south
were the rapids. Immediately below, along the river, hundreds of
canoes moved gently in the current, guarded by Indians not eligible
to attend the conclave.

Indians sat in two groups, the Iroquois on the governor's
right, the Algonquins on his left. The governor and his party completed a circle of a sort, and if any Frenchman's heart quaked,
he did not show it. The Indians were dressed in their frightening
best. On their heads were fastened skulls of buffalo or elk—horns
thrust high. Their faces seemed unreal under coats of brilliant

paint. Necklaces of bones and teeth hung low. Human scalps of many shades dangled from their belts.

When all were seated the governor waited, letting the tension grow. In time, he rose and took a few steps forward; the sun sparkled on his jewels and shone on the satin of his brilliant court dress.

Then he began to speak, making an impassioned plea for peace. The Indians followed the rise and fall of his voice. When he finished, there was silence until he motioned for the translator to begin. During this repetition of his speech, the governor stood motionless, eyeing the listeners. All this pleased the Indians; the Frenchman gave them the importance they wanted.

When the interpreter ended, the governor took two steps forward and picked up a hatchet which was lying there ready. He lifted it high, glanced around to make sure he held every eye, then shouted:

"I would dig a pit so deep that the bottom could never be found! I would toss this hatchet into it—and you would toss yours. And never again would Frenchmen and Indians war with each other!" He hurled the hatchet into the ground before him and held his defiant pose, waiting as the Indians roared approval.

Of course, the conclave was not over. The representative of each tribe must have his chance at oratory. The sun was setting over the Ottawa when the last man finished and peace pipes glowed in the long twilight. Everyone, though exhausted, seemed content. Frontenac would have been proud and pleased.

For many years there was peace—peace, that is, with the Indians. No conclave could change economic facts. The English Hudson's Bay Company flourished on the north; the English settlers to the south moved on westward toward the mountains; and both the English and the French wanted furs for Europe.

But few people in the New World gave thought to such matters. Life along the river was pleasanter each year. Now families came from France, and each wanted a place on the river; sometimes farms were very narrow and stretched back four and five miles toward the forests. Ships brought news and some comforts.

The resumption of the fur trade meant that *coureurs de bois* and *voyageurs* returned each spring with loads of fur. Admiring crowds greeted them; their colorful capotes, fringed leggings, and gay stocking caps marked them as men of the wilderness. Their tales of far up the lakes, beyond Sault Ste. Marie, were listened to eagerly and gave a hint—but only a hint—of the vast length of the great waterway. Occasionally a trader came by the lower lakes and the St. Lawrence. But most still used the Ottawa route; it was shorter, and while it had rapids, it had none like the Long Sault— miles of danger, with many a bateau wrecked and cargo lost. Nothing was done to make more little canals. The one near Montreal had limited use and had been difficult to dig.

Meanwhile a Montreal Frenchman, Iberville, had founded a village on the Mississippi which he called New Orleans. La Salle would have been pleased with this; it was what he had intended to do himself. A few forts were built farther up on the Mississippi. The English gave no evidence that they noticed.

Then word came to the governor of the Virginia colony that the French, with their Indian allies, had moved up the St. Lawrence, up the lakes to the southern shores of Lake Erie. They claimed land as far south as the Ohio River.

Lake Erie! Ohio River! Those were strange new words in Virginia. The governor should send someone to tell the French to move back; this was English land.

CHAPTER 4

A Foundation Laid

GEORGE Washington, then twenty-one years old and a surveyor, did his first service to his "country"—that is, the colony and the king—when he went to Williamsburg and volunteered to take that long wilderness journey to Fort Le Boeuf near Lake Erie. He had acquired considerable knowledge of wilderness in connection with his work, but he did not know how far away the fort was. It proved to be five hundred and sixty miles. He did know the journey would be hard, but he liked adventure.

The commandant at Fort Le Boeuf was polite and formal. He read the letter Washington brought and assured the young man that all this Ohio country belonged to France. If he wanted to present his case, he must go to the governor at Quebec. Washington

had no orders to go to Quebec. He accepted a letter from the commandant to the governor of Virginia and set out on the return
journey over ice and snow, in the bitter cold.

The real French answer was the strengthening of Fort Niagara
and of Fort Duquesne at the head of the Ohio River. The contest
continued as it had for years; the prize was the profitable fur trade.
Governors of northern English colonies planned a conference "for
mutual safety." But the meeting at Albany in 1754 had no result.
Colonies would not work together, not even for mutual defense.

The British, aroused at last, sent royal troops under General
Braddock to wipe out the forts near the colonies; instead, the king's
troops were slaughtered, the general killed. Three years later the
French, finding that the position at the Ohio was too difficult to
hold, burned the fort and left. Young Washington and his colonials
saw the smoke of that fire and felt cheated of a real victory. They
rebuilt the fort and named it Fort Pitt. The city of Pittsburgh has
now made a beautiful Memorial Park on that site at the junction
of the rivers which form the Ohio.

The contest between the French and the British was not
settled below the lakes, as Washington hoped, but on the St. Lawrence River in the summer of 1759. An English fleet with General
Wolfe aboard moved up the St. Lawrence River to take Quebec.
The general studied that huge rock in despair; how could he take
such a place? Travelers today ask the same question; that rock seems
impregnable. General Wolfe looked again, and noticed women washing clothes by the edge of the river. Rather idly, he swept his glass
up. Then he straightened his shoulders. What were those white
things spread on low bushes along the top of the rock? Clean
laundry? How did laundry get there if no path led up the rock? He
studied the rock again; he spied a moving figure, a woman dressed
in black carrying something white under her arm.

Spies confirmed his guess that the French got food supplies

up that same winding path. Why couldn't his men be mistaken for
food carriers and climb the rock? An attack at dawn resulted. Two
brave generals, Wolfe and the French Montcalm, were killed along
with many others, but the battle won New France for England.

Final peace papers, signed in 1763, gave all the upper part of
North America to the English—an area called Canada. But along
the river, the French stayed French. By their daily living they set
up a resistance more effective than battle. The English, wisely as it
proved, yielded. The French retained their language, their civil
law, and their church. The English, in the main, settled on up the
river in thinly populated areas and kept their language, their law,
their church.

Far to the south from the St. Lawrence, friction grew worse
between England and her colonies. Benjamin Franklin was sent to
England in the hope of working out better relations. While in
Europe he visited France and became a friend of many notable
Frenchmen whose ideals seemed like his own. Could these people,
he wondered, possibly be happy under English rule in Canada?

On his return to Philadelphia in 1775, with the war of rebellion
already begun, he heard that same question asked. Willingly he
accepted an appointment to go with two others and invite French
Canadians to join in the rebellion and to become the fourteenth
state in the new nation.

The Canadian French declined. True, they were technically
under the English. But they were doing very well; would they be
certain to do better in a new nation? Regretfully the commission
returned home. But they left behind one enduring cultural gift, a
printing press.

Franklin always liked printed, rather than longhand records.
He had brought with him a skilled printer, Fleury Mesplet, and a
printing press which he helped to set up in the basement of the
Chateau de Ramezey where the commission was housed. When the

conference ended, Mesplet chose to stay in Montreal; he liked the place. He started a newspaper, a weekly *Gazette*, said to be the first newspaper in Canada, and it continues to this day.

The war lasted eight years, and in the end the United States of America was recognized as a free and independent nation. It might seem that all this was far removed from the St. Lawrence and the Great Lakes. But actually, in two ways the future of the vast waterway was vitally affected.

First, the boundary line settled by the treaty of Versailles in 1783 gave to Canada the whole vast upper portion of North America. The boundary was along the 49th parallel to Lake Superior between Port Arthur and Duluth, down the middle of four lakes to the St. Lawrence, down the river through the Long Sault. Below these rapids the international line cuts east over the hills to the sea. Lake Michigan is the only lake entirely bounded by one nation; all the rest of the world's greatest waterway is shared—a fact that was to grow in significance.

The second result of importance to the waterway area was the great migration of Loyalists, also called Tories, from the United States to Canada. This began even before peace was signed, grew steadily for more than a decade, and did not end for many years.

Many a man and his family, bound by traditional ties of loyalty to the English crown, to relatives, to business, had considered the rebellion in the colonies a passing madness in which they had no part. Others, used to considering themselves English, joined English troops to fight for the mother country. By the end of the war these Loyalists had lost everything—houses, lands, businesses, friends, and often their own relatives, whose devotion to a new ideal of freedom and a new form of government had changed the course of history.

Those who lived near the sea went to England or to Nova Scotia. Loyalists further inland crossed the St. Lawrence to settle

along the Thousand Islands or on the Island of Quinté, or the
peninsula west of Lake Ontario. Others crossed that strip to settle
on the northern shores of Lake Ontario or Lake Erie. Many of the
migrants had been well-to-do; now they had lost everything. They
walked on this journey, carrying what they could. The strong sur-
vived to help make a nation.

In 1791 the political form of Canada altered. The French portion became Lower Canada—lower, that is, down river. The English
part was Upper Canada, southwest, up the St. Lawrence.

By this time Canadians had begun to realize the value of their
new citizens—and also their poverty. The new government gave
two hundred acres of land to a family, some livestock, often staple
food, and a little clothing.

Before the end of the eighteenth century, more people began
migrating from Europe, too, especially Scots. Some families, who
were not Loyalists, moved west from Pennsylvania, met the Indian
terror in Ohio, and crossed over to Canada. Upper Canada grew
rapidly.

Ohioans fought and won the Battle of Fallen Timbers on the
Maumee River, near Toledo, in 1793. The conquered Indians were
forced west and never again were they a major threat to settlements
or to commerce along the Great Lakes-St. Lawrence Waterway.

For eighty years after that first little canal near Montreal was
dug, nothing, so far as is known, was done to improve water transport. In 1780, a few shallow, narrow canals were made to bypass
difficult spots on the St. Lawrence. These were for the fur trade and
too small to admit bateaux loaded with passengers. In 1797 the
North West Fur Company built a canal and locks on the north
shore at Sault Ste. Marie. Oxen pulled bateaux through the canal
approaches; men opened and shut the wooden gates by hand-
operated windlass. The lift in the lock chamber was about nine feet.
That was less than half of the twenty-one foot fall of the rapids, but

it helped. A replica of this lock has been built near its original location. Together with the blockhouse nearby, it is an interesting reminder of those early days. But it is so small that many visitors fail to recognize it as a lock. It is thought of as a little fish pond!

These efforts were far apart and accomplished little. Yet they did keep thought of a waterway in the public mind, and the idea of improvement did not quite die. As farms were cleared and larger crops gathered, people all along the lower lakes and the river looked for a market.

Transport across the lakes was usually by Durham boat—a sturdy craft with pointed bow and square stern, or by Mackinaw boat—pointed at both bow and stern. Such a craft was rowed or sailed and could take a good-sized load. Few settlers used birch-bark canoes, but even their sturdier boats would be inadequate for the commerce hoped for in a few years.

Both the United States and Canada were beginning to think seriously about transport when suddenly they were at war—and with each other! Unrelated resentments had led to this war: impressment of American sailors by England; the persistent feeling of some people in the United States that if invaded, Canada would be glad to join the United States; and many other irritations and jealousies.

So Canada was invaded—and repulsed the invaders. Up along the St. Marys River, Americans took Mackinac Island and Canadians destroyed the canal and lock at Sault Ste. Marie and most of the village south of the rapids. Americans burned the Parliament buildings at York, and British burned the White House at Washington. It was a useless, tit-for-tat war, a war that changed no boundaries. But it did have results.

The two sections of Canada, Upper and Lower, had met a common enemy, and, having repulsed the invader, began to feel a unity that never before had seemed possible. The two languages, two courts, two churches, continued. But the people felt united; they were Canadians. The United States learned that this new Canada meant to be herself; she was not a joiner of another nation. Both nations saw that their best good lay in mutual respect and acceptance.

This ideal has had its moments of challenge but, though at times strained, has held and has grown steadily, to the good fortune of both the United States of America and the Dominion of Canada. The long, undefended frontier is evidence all the world can see. By the middle of the twentieth century this foundation of trust had become so solid that the two nations could co-operate in constructing a power installation and a seaway with shared plans, shared costs, shared use—an entirely new and a very heartening aspect in international relations.

CHAPTER 5

A Bold New Idea

EVEN before the War of 1812, people in the region of the lower lakes began to enjoy a feeling of prosperity. Farmers had larger fields and grew more than they needed for themselves; a few small industries developed, mostly sawmills, grain mills, and potash works. But neighbors had this same kind of produce, the same surplus; markets must be found in lake towns where lumber, flour, and potash were needed.

Lake transport was seriously handicapped—as in the days of Frontenac and La Salle—by Niagara Falls and the peninsula with the high escarpment. Boats could not get from one lake to the other, and twenty-eight miles of portage was slow and costly. The more business grew, the more frustrating this natural barrier became; but there seemed nothing to be done about it.

By 1815, soldiers of both countries had left the service and returned home—none more happily than William Hamilton Merritt of St. Catharines, a town near Lake Ontario and a few miles from Port Niagara. During the last part of the war, Hamilton had been held in a prison camp in Massachusetts. Now he was newly married to the daughter of a New York senator and was determined to make a success of his life. His father was a Loyalist from Westchester County, New York, who had migrated to the Niagara Peninsula in 1796 when Hamilton was three years old. Like most boys of his day, the son had little formal education; he had clerked in his father's store at St. Catharines and had been in service since the beginning of the war. Those experiences and chores on his father's farm were all the preparation he had, but his dreams were of big enterprises.

Young Merritt began at once to build a good house and a general store, both in St. Catharines. He bought a farm by Twelve Mile Creek, a little stream that flowed by his own and his father's farms and emptied into Lake Ontario near St. Catharines. He built a dam across this creek and on his land he put up a flour mill "with three run of stone," a distillery, a potashery, a cooper shop, a smithy, and five houses for his employees. These buildings were not yet finished when he began to dig a salt mine and to plan marketing salt in a big way.

Of course he had no money to pay for all this building; he was young and just out of the army and prison camp. And his diary says frankly, "I understand no branch of the many businesses in which I am engaged."

But Hamilton Merritt had two qualities more important just then than money; he had ideas, and he had confidence in himself. Post-war years brought boom times both to Canada and to the United States. Men talked about "making the place hum!"— wherever that place might be. Merritt had no trouble in borrowing money, and he plunged ahead.

The next year, as these various businesses were getting under way, Merritt's sister married Charles Ingersoll, a man who served under Merritt in the war. The two men liked and trusted each other. They formed a partnership. Merritt had imagination and a driving energy; Ingersoll had intelligence and steadiness. Both were hard workers. Neither gave a thought to their mounting debts. Their story at the start was like that of many ambitious young men of their day.

Merritt left Ingersoll in charge of final building operations and went to Montreal, Quebec, and New York, to buy merchandise for the store. His purchases would be on credit, of course, but that was easy for a young man of his ability to get. Business along the St. Lawrence was founded on the fur trade, and that required long credits. At best a trader "came down" only once a year. After a bad season his account must be carried along two or three years until he could pay off with a good season.

Then, too, the number and importance of the general stores had grown as Upper Canada developed. With transport so very difficult, the only way a farmer could get some staples was through a store—not too far away. In the 1780's, trade had been by barter, the farmer paying in wheat or potash. After the war some currency was in circulation, and it was easier to do business.

Soon after Merritt's return, merchandise began to arrive. The partners parceled it out and sent small lots to various little settlements along the peninsula. When possible, goods were sent by boat along the shore; trails and poor roads must ascend that high escarpment to get to farm communities higher up.

The firm of Merritt and Ingersoll prospered. Much of their success was based on the mills on Twelve Mile Creek. Farmers brought produce there and spent their credits at the main store. The grist mill was especially profitable because flour was easier to transport to Montreal than wheat and brought a higher cash price.

The partners were beginning to need cash to pay interest on their debts.

Of course this whole business structure depended upon water in Twelve Mile Creek—but water had been there since as far back as anyone could remember. It was such a sure thing that no one mentioned it; no one thought to appreciate its value.

When Merritt came home from a buying trip in the late summer of 1818, he was shocked to find that this pattern of success had been abruptly stopped. The creek was dry. The mills were silent. Other mills along the creek were still; other millers were in serious trouble.

"In the spring we have freshets—floods, really—that break down the dams," a neighbor complained to Merritt. "We fix the dams, and now we have no water."

No one mentioned that clearing forests from the land higher up to plant orchards and wheat might have let the spring rains run off instead of being held in the soil as heretofore. People only saw that something must be done to save the business community; they looked to Merritt for ideas.

Hopefully, Merritt and two or three others climbed the escarpment, that steep formation that many called a hill or a mountain. It was neither; it went up and remained on the high level of the rest of the peninsula some 326 feet above Lake Ontario. Merritt saw that the ravine and springs that fed Twelve Mile Creek were dry. But on the higher level, two rivers, the Welland and the Grand, and several creeks could be glimpsed from a ridge beyond the top of the escarpment.

"A ditch from the Welland would bring water to the ravine," Merritt suggested, as they looked to him.

"How would you get it over this ridge?" one of his companions asked.

"It's not more than thirty feet high. We could tunnel through." Now that Merritt had an idea, his mind worked fast. That ridge was at least sixty feet high, but what was the difference—thirty, sixty? "Let's make a survey. Then we can get at the work quickly." By the time they had tramped back to the mills, their plans were formed.

A survey of a sort was made, and some time in the next two

weeks the word "canal" instead of "ditch" began to be used. On the fourteenth of October, 1818, a formal petition to dig a canal was presented to a public meeting in Niagara. It is not clear who first used that word canal, or when. But the record shows that Merritt used it most effectively. There was a newness, a boldness about digging a canal and conveying boats up a hill as well as water down a ravine that seemed to fit the people's desperate need —and Merritt's temperament.

The plan had several parts. A canal would float boats to the foot of the escarpment. There a slide—some called it a railway—would allow boats to be hauled up or eased down by oxen or men. On the top a tunnel through the ridge would open into a canal to the Welland River. The Welland flowed into the Niagara. From there, a boat could go on to Lake Erie, as La Salle's *Griffin* had done so long before. This ambitious plan, grown from the need to get water to run mills, shows the quickness of Merritt's mind and imagination.

Many thought the idea fantastic, even laughable. But it had a very practical aspect to a man who had traveled as much as Merritt had. By this time several short canals supplemented by rivers bypassed difficult places on the St. Lawrence River. In the Allegheny Mountains, especially in Pennsylvania, there were several "slides" where men or oxen hauled small boats up to a higher level. To be sure, such movement was dangerous. Manpower sometimes failed; ropes that looked strong broke; there were many accidents. John Roebling's first important invention in 1841 was to be wire rope to replace more fragile rope on such slides. But when a slide was satisfactory, merchandise was moved more quickly and at considerable profit.

If such a slide could be constructed, and along with it a ditch to bring water to the mills, St. Catharines would have quick prosperity. At the last minute a paragraph was added to the petition requesting permission to build three locks if any were needed.

Talk about the petition naturally got across Niagara River to New York State, where people were already interested in the Erie Canal. This canal, which was to connect Albany and Buffalo, was still in the planning stage in 1818 and was often called "Clinton's Ditch." It appeared likely that the canal would go straight to Buffalo, south of towns along Lake Ontario. If Merritt could get his plans approved and the work done in two years, as he said, he would beat the Erie Canal and take merchandise to and from Lake Erie and Montreal.

From the first talk about the Erie Canal, Canadians had realized that if it bypassed Lake Ontario and opened up the other three lakes with cheap transport to New York, the port of Montreal and towns on Lake Ontario would be crippled. Farmers and merchants who had come to the October meeting favored Merritt's petition.

But the town of Niagara was the center of a thriving portage business, and every portage man was there to protect his living. Without this quick, vigorous opposition, the petition might have been accepted. Instead, it failed. Later, Merritt could not even appeal to the government, because political troubles in Lower Canada blocked payment of funds to Upper Canada, and the government had no money for new projects. Fall rains brought some water down Twelve Mile Creek, and people soon forgot that the mills had stopped.

Then, suddenly the postwar boom ended. A terrible depression set in, affecting every family. Merritt was bankrupt.

By 1821, the government of Lower Canada, recovering, began to construct a new canal with locks to bypass the Lachine Rapids and bring trade down the river to the port of Montreal. In four years this canal was in service. The new canal was 4½ feet deep with seven locks 100 feet long and 20 feet wide; the hand-operated wooden gates were the best then known. This canal was so successful that eighteen years later its capacity was doubled. Upper Canada, challenged by this canal, began plans for a canal across the peninsula; but nothing was actually begun.

Hamilton Merritt was not defeated by the general depression. Surprisingly soon he had his affairs in order, and backed by the money and faith of relatives and friends, he revived plans for a waterway. Upper Canada's ideas for a canal did not please him. It was far from St. Catharines; such a canal would not help him or his neighbors. He revived his earlier plans and began to buy up pieces of land which he thought would increase in value and pay for the hard work he saw ahead.

At a meeting of St. Catharines people, Merritt proposed to build a canal by their town at a cost of $10,000. People cheered and pledged money for a survey at once. The survey estimated the cost at three times Merritt's figure, plus $20,000 if his newest idea—locks to float boats up the escarpment—was used. The matter might have died then, but for a feeling of urgency: the Erie Canal was pushing westward. Everyone knew what disaster *that* would bring to Ontario ports. They listened to Merritt.

He planned a canal 4 feet deep, the same as the Erie. Locks would bypass the mills and carry boats up the escarpment. There the canal would go through the ridge and on to the Welland River, to the Niagara River, and to Lake Erie. Water for the section up the escarpment would come from the Welland River. Some day another canal might go beyond the Welland to the Grand River and through its good harbor into Lake Erie.

The daring of the plan was breathtaking. Merritt was a promoter, not an engineer; he had conceived of navigation up a 326-foot grade—a feat never even approached before. If he could succeed, he would take the first and perhaps the most important step toward a connected waterway from Duluth to the sea.

Upper Canada gave Merritt a charter. No one questioned the

depth proposed, 4 feet, nor his plans nor costs, nor the time—one year. He did not ask for money; he meant to raise private capital. Jubilantly he began work: he must organize the Welland Canal Company, raise funds, hire technical men and workmen for the construction. He began all this in February, 1824, as the Erie Canal was pushing westward.

Merritt was an honest, skilled promoter, giving his time— profit on his properties was a gamble, dependent on the canal's success. But investors were fearful of such a new idea. After weeks in Toronto, Montreal, and Quebec, he had raised only about a quarter of the money needed. He went to New York, and there found plenty of investors.

"Your canal will help all of us, not just Canadians," several men said. "The Erie's nearly finished. Two canals will be better than one. Competition is good for trade. How much do you need?"

To New Yorkers, the difficulties seemed trifling. The canal was to be only 28 miles long—look at the Erie, 360 miles at least! Merritt explained about the 326-foot escarpment, but few listened, and fewer had any idea of the geography of that peninsula. They liked the idea of building a canal with private funds. All through the nineteenth century men risked loss on the chance of profit as they opened up the country with canals, railroads, highways, and industries.

Confident at last that he would have money, Merritt went upstate, along the Erie Canal, to inform himself about labor and equipment. He needed engineers and foremen, hundreds of work-men; plows, harrows, hand shovels, ox teams. Most of all he had to learn what he did need.

He was amazed at the welcome given him. Then he realized that, with the Erie Canal nearing completion, men were glad to get jobs nearby. Contractors offered to take part pay in stock. They believed in canals, and Merritt's was a thrilling new venture. Fifty

bids were made for various parts of the work. In November, the
first contract was signed, and five days later work began on that
tunnel into the ridge on the higher level.

Directors of the company and others attended simple ceremonies of "first digging." Even then, many had begun to guess that
there must be some changes of plan. The government wanted a
deeper canal; 4 feet was too shallow to have military value, and it
was still remembered that two fleets had been needed on the lakes
in the recent war. Port towns along Ontario fought for the canal
entrance. If the town of Niagara, instead of St. Catharines, got the
entrance, Merritt and many neighbors would lose all chance of
profit on their land and businesses.

Meanwhile the digging went well. Gangs worked from both
sides of the ridge on that 16-foot tunnel. Visitors climbed up daily
to watch the work—the scene was inspiring.

Then suddenly the middle of the tunnel was flooded as hidden
springs were tapped. Men fled for their lives. Never again would a
workman enter that wrecked tunnel! The entire plan for conquering
that ridge must be changed, or the project dropped.

Faith in Merritt and his bold idea collapsed.

"How did he ever think he could make boats climb a hill?"
people said, and shook their heads, amazed at their own credulity.

Behind closed doors, the directors met to consider their
changed situation. Now, in the dead of winter, with thousands of
their own and other men's dollars spent and nothing to show for
it, they would have to make new plans, raise more money, and
somehow find new faith to start over.

And, even as they met, the Erie Canal was coming nearer to
Buffalo and to Lake Erie.

CHAPTER 6

The Welland Canal

THE citizens of St. Catharines were
much pleased with the new charter that the Welland Canal Company signed in February of 1825. The route was settled—Twelve
Mile Creek by St. Catharines and to the nearby Port Dalhousie on
Lake Ontario—and the charter provided for locks around the mill
dams. This charter seemed to assure good business for St. Catharines
merchants and high values for local real estate.

The canal was to be larger, too, than the one planned earlier,
and that would attract investors. Thirty-five wooden locks were to
lift or lower schooners, sloops, and small craft at the escarpment.
The directors knew that stone locks would be better than wood, but
they had no money for stone work—and no time to install stone;

early opening seemed more important. Wooden locks would last a few years and prove the value of the project. The depth was to be 7½ feet; width at surface 54 feet and 34 feet at bottom.

In place of the tunnel at the ridge there was to be a canal called "Deep Cut," ambitiously dug through the ridge to the Welland River. The bottom of Deep Cut must be below the level of the Welland River, because water for the locks and canal to Twelve Mile Creek must come from that river. This water supply was essential; Merritt did not forget that lack of water for his mills had started his entire project.

"Once we get to the Welland River, our problems will end," the directors told each other confidently. That river had a good and steady supply of water and was navigable for thirty miles, only the last eight of which were needed for the canal's final stretch to the Niagara River, above the falls.

The directors knew that there were two objections to this route: the swift current above the falls and the ice jams late each spring at the Niagara River's head in Lake Erie. This whole river was an unusual formation that had so long isolated the peninsula— swift currents with ice jams in spring; then the falls where tons of water leaped half the 326-foot drop in one stunning roar; then whirlpools and rapids on to Lake Ontario. Timid directors feared that a boat might get through the canal only to swirl down and over the falls!

"We'll conquer the current by providing strong ox teams and a towpath all the way to Lake Erie," a bolder director said.

"Give us time," another proposed, "and we'll dig another canal, to the Grand River, where ice doesn't mass as at Niagara." This alternative plan would please the government, too. Grand River had a good harbor and was farther from the United States border—a point still important to some Canadians.

Labor problems seemed to lighten suddenly as men came and

applied for work. The Erie Canal was to open in October of 1825; some sections were already finished. Contractors, foremen, and unskilled workmen were eager to work on the peninsula.

"We'll have the canal done as far as the Welland by spring of '27," contractors promised. "We've had experience with canals, you see." No one seemed to realize that their experience was quite unlike the present job; soil and grades on the peninsula were very different from those encountered in digging the Erie Canal, along which the many streams across New York State provided ample water.

The work got under way, and during 1826 went steadily ahead. The canal to the escarpment with its locks by the mills was dug. The thirty-five locks up the escarpment were built. As the work pushed on, the fame of the project spread. Visitors made special trips to watch the construction. The whole area stirred with activity as hundreds of workmen dug earth, loaded it into wheelbarrows, or put it into sacks flung across their shoulders, and moved it away. A million and a half cubic feet of earth was moved—nothing like this had ever been seen or imagined before! Miles of canal banks were neatly finished; towpaths were made. The whole project seemed a miracle of construction.

"It's mighty different from the Erie," a traveler was quoted as saying. "Even when I stand here and look at it, I can't see how a boat is going to climb up that mountain!"

Of course the locks in the ravine were still dry; no cofferdam was needed. There would be no water until the Welland River was tapped; Deep Cut, a mile and a half long, must be dug before water would fill the locks.

The year 1827 came—spring, summer, and fall passed, and all was well. The canal from Lake Ontario to St. Catharines was opened and became popular at once for import and export near the lake. Merchants were delighted with increased business; small

craft came right up to St. Catharines. The place had grown in two
years, and everyone was prosperous and proud of the canal.

Work on Deep Cut began, but went slowly. The kind of earth
to be removed proved difficult and unlike what the contractors
had expected. A cash prize of the enormous sum of 125 pounds was
offered for any equipment that would speed the work.

Oliver Phelps, a subcontractor, won that prize for a contrivance
that was considered a miracle. Phelps rigged a strong timber with a
pulley at one end. Over the pulley he ran a chain with a bucket at

A pictorial diagram of Niagara Peninsula, showing the escarpment.

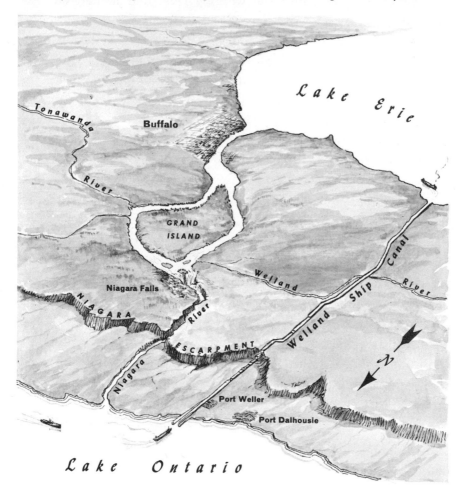

each end. He planted the timber up the slope above the digging. As one bucket was filled, it dropped down and was emptied into sacks and the earth carried off. The dropping of one bucket sent the "empty" up for refilling; this gravity process saved men clambering up and down the slope. It seems to be the first recorded labor-saving device in canal construction. Phelps won not only the prize but a promotion. Still, when bad weather began, Deep Cut was not finished.

Winter was unusually cold, and spring was late. Money was vanishing as delay used up capital. Someone found a spring, and contractors let water into the working level and floated out excavated material on hastily improvised scows.

Autumn came. Workmen agreed to take pay in notes—a kind of scrip or promise to pay later—which local merchants agreed to honor so the men could eat. Contractors took all pay in stock.

A cold wind was blowing one day when Merritt went up from town to see how work was going.

"Two weeks more will see us through," a contractor called.

"I hope you are right!" Merritt called back, fervently, and walked on.

Suddenly, above the hum of work, he heard an odd rumble—a frightening sound because it was strange and new.

"Help! Help!" Shrill screams of terror came from a gang of men working on down the cut; then, pitiful, panting cries as men raced for their lives. Merritt turned in time to see the raw slopes of Deep Cut sliding down on the gang of workmen. From the whole length of the Cut, men raced to give help. Beating at the sliding earth with their hands, they pulled away screaming men, dug out the injured, and searched to make sure all were out. Luckily the worst of the slide was behind the largest gangs of workmen. It appeared that no lives were lost.

Hours later, when there was time to appraise the damage and

discover a cause, men were still shaking from the terror of their escape.

"The banks are too steep," a contractor suggested. "We should have foreseen that."

"But, look! What's this?"

Several men were standing at the edge of the slide. One rubbed his shoe along the bottom. . . . "Quicksand," he cried. *"Quicksand!"*

"If we've struck quicksand, we'll never finish Deep Cut," another exclaimed. He turned to a crowd of workmen waiting near. "No more work today!" he shouted. They hurried off, glad to leave the place.

This second disaster on the ridge showed the directors that a cut could not be dug deep enough to bring water from the Welland River level to the head of the ravine. Several engineers made new plans. The one accepted was an odd one—bold, too. But it worked. The proposal was to raise the level of the Grand River by a dam well up from the harbor; build a feeder canal and aqueduct; bring water from the Grand *over* the Welland and, at a new higher level, through Deep Cut to the ravine. Much of the earth so laboriously dug and moved must be brought back to Deep Cut to bury the quicksand, and two new pairs of locks must be built to lift and lower craft at the higher level of Deep Cut.

More money was raised; the work was renewed. The feeder canal brought plenty of water. The locks lifted craft, and the water easily floated vessels into the Welland River.

Formal ceremonies had been planned for the day when the first vessels went through between the lakes, but work was delayed. It was the last day in November of 1829 and very cold, when two schooners, the American *W. H. Boughton,* and the Canadian *Jane and Anne,* passed through—the first ships ever to go between Lake Erie and Lake Ontario.

Histories do not agree upon the date of the opening of the

Welland Canal—this day in 1829 is used, but some give 1830, 1831, 1832, or 1833. This disagreement is not surprising; 1827 might be used, too, for then the first stretch to St. Catharines began to be used. In each of the years recorded, some section of the canal was opened, or altered and reopened. In one sense, the canal has never been finished, for it has been continually improved and enlarged.

All through the years of struggle and construction, objectors were very free with talk **against** the whole project. False rumors

were spread: the opening was postponed, the opening had to wait a year; labor troubles would make completion of the canal impossible. . . . Such gossip had been continuous since the first decision to have the canal pass St. Catharines had been announced. It deterred ship owners from planning to use the canal and cost the Canal Company much business at a time when they needed every cent they could earn. People in other towns felt jealous and annoyed and spoke of the canal as a failure.

That Welland Canal was not a failure. It encountered many difficulties that would be avoided at a later day, but it was the first imaginative move to build a connected waterway from the Great Lakes to the sea. It served the craft of the time well, and its very defects spurred men's thinking about canals and waterways. With the worst natural barrier—Niagara Falls—bypassed, there was more than hope; there was actual expectation that the rapids at Sault Ste. Marie and the difficult reaches of the St. Lawrence River could be overcome, too.

Among many who foresaw a waterway, perhaps none had more influence than a Canadian, the Honorable John Young of Montreal. In 1825, when the Erie Canal was opened and the building of the Welland Canal was under way, he began to promote the idea of a St. Lawrence seaway. By 1832, with the Welland successfully locking vessels up and down the escarpment, Young published an article on inland navigation; he wrote convincingly about a through seaway connecting all the lakes with the Atlantic Ocean.

Merritt's brilliant accomplishment, Young's vision, brought no immediate results. But they sowed an idea—long in germinating, but richly fruitful as time gave it the chance to grow.

CHAPTER 7

Decades of Change

PUBLIC enthusiasm for canals grew rapidly through the 1830's and 1840's. Canada built the very useful Rideau Canal, linking several small lakes and rivers to make a waterway from Ottawa to Lake Ontario. The first Beauharnois Canal was opened in 1845; canals above and below Cornwall and the Galop Canal were opened at about that same time. By 1847 the state of Ohio had finished digging most of the 400 miles of canals planned; Indiana, Illinois, and other states were working hard to give their people the cheap water transport needed to get products to markets.

Such transport had become a necessity, for during these same decades, thousands of Europeans migrated to North America, both to the United States and to Canada. Vast numbers of these people arrived with the idea of going west to settle; from New York, they went up the Hudson, on by the Erie Canal and then by sailing ships on the Great Lakes. Those who landed at Quebec or Montreal did not as yet have the smooth three-mile-an-hour transport the Erie Canal provided; canals along the St. Lawrence were not connected and were more useful for carrying cargo than people. A man named Alexander Sinclair wrote an account of his family's arrival in Montreal from Scotland and of their journey up the St. Lawrence River to Prescott. He was a boy of twelve then, but he never forgot the adventures and hardships of that trip. He wrote:

"The spring of 1831, my father sold the farm and everything except what we could take to America, which consisted of clothes, dishes and books. . . . On the first of May-we went to Greenoch where we waited until an immigrant ship with room for us arrived. . . . The *Tamerline* set sail down the river and we bade good-by forever to all our kin and friends. . . . Most of the passengers were sick and on account of head winds we were seven weeks and two days crossing and coming to Quebec. The views along the river were beautiful and French farmers came to the ship to sell us vegetables.

"A large steamer came alongside and took passengers and their luggage for Montreal. From there we took barges or long boats to Prescott. Each barge or boat had six Frenchmen with pikes and oars to push or row the boat. It was then that I first saw oxen working. In coming up the rapids, they tied a long rope to the boat and hitched the oxen to the rope while the men with pikes kept the boat off the rocks. It took nearly two weeks between Montreal and Prescott."

During this long and dangerous journey passengers and crew slept on shore at night, rolled in blankets—if they had blankets with them. So many immigrants traveled this route that some farmers gave up farming for the more profitable work of dragging boats at the edge of the rapids.

At Prescott the travelers got a steamer for Toronto. Steamers of the early 1830's were very elegant, with a "parlour" and long rows of "couches" along the walls; passengers could rest if the trip was long. Compared with a blanket on a rock, this was luxury.

These were prosperous years in America; people were full of ambition and hope. Andrew Jackson, the first frontier president of the United States, was interested in the West, as George Washington and Thomas Jefferson had been before him. In the 1830's, even professional men and businessmen talked about going West, and some really went.

Young Cyrus McCormick, in the wheat state of Virginia, invented a reaping machine. He also originated an entirely new method of selling his machine; he was willing to deliver a reaper after a small down payment. A farmer then dared to plant several times the number of acres that could be reaped by hand and pay for his reaper when his crop was sold. McCormick's invention and his new way of selling enabled many a family to risk moving out to rich prairie land around and beyond the Great Lakes.

This movement of people required ships and houses—even small cabins needed lumber. Roads, such as they were, required cutting trees. Some areas made corduroy roads, logs laid at right angles to the direction of the road. These could be made quickly because the middle-sized trees used were plentiful and relatively easy to cut and handle; but travel on corduroy was rough and tiring. Other areas made plank roads of sawed lumber. Of course there were plenty of trees. Lower Michigan was believed to have more trees than could ever be used by man—fine hardwood south, good pine to the north of the lower peninsula. Wood was wasted recklessly. Good logs of hard timber were burned to clear a field.

"There's plenty," people said. "Plenty of everything in America!" All this was very well for settlers along Lake Huron, Lake Michigan, and the lower lakes. Land around and beyond Lake

Superior was said to be good; the fishing there was profitable too. But the mile of rapids at Sault Ste. Marie was a barrier. Reapers and household goods, stoves, chests, and other general cargo could not be taken up the rapids in birchbark canoes. And how could crops be brought down? These things, so unlike soft, compact furs, were difficult to portage, too, though a portage business had begun to develop.

In the year Michigan became a state, 1837, there was some talk and effort to build a canal along the south shore of the rapids and bypass its dangers; if some federal aid were granted, the work could be done. This hope was reasonable because the federal government was interested in "internal improvements" just then—canals, highways, railroads. But in congress, Henry Clay made an impassioned speech against spending money so far away. He ended with his famous sentence, "I would as soon think of building a canal on the moon!"

Michigan, her pride challenged, resolved to build the canal herself and open a waterway to her own northern shore. Portage people at Sault Ste. Marie objected, but plans were drawn, a contractor engaged, workmen hired, money paid out. Then an earnest officer, on duty at the fort at the Sault, discovered that Michigan's route for the canal cut through federal land by the fort. He used troops to halt the work.

There was a rumor that the contractor was glad to hurry away as he had bid too low. Anyway, he left, taking with him money he had been paid. Portage people smiled smugly. Fifteen years passed before people generally knew enough about northern Michigan and Lake Superior to listen to the idea of a waterway through to this greatest of freshwater lakes.

People in the United States and Canada in general had no interest in happenings at Sault Ste. Marie. The few who may have heard that the canal project was abandoned probably agreed with

Henry Clay in thinking of the place as too remote to be important; there was none of the feeling of immediacy that had helped push through the Welland and other canals.

The Indians had long since learned to live with the rapids, as they had learned to navigate the Ottawa and the St. Lawrence rivers. Their skill and courage got the furs down and brought trade goods up on the return voyages. Few others ventured on the St. Marys River.

The villages by the rapids remained unchanged for years—half Indian, half American on the south shore; half Indian, half French in the little settlement on the north shore.

Then suddenly all that changed.

The era of prosperity ended in a deep depression. Men who had never been tempted by glowing tales of the West now thought of adventuring because they could not make a living where they were. Soon they and their families were on the move, by horse, mule, or ox teams. Others went by canal and lakes; still others walked, carrying what they could, saving their meager cash to buy land. The movement was opposite in direction from the Algonquin migration so long before, and it was vigorous and swift.

A second factor in the sudden change was the abrupt failure of the fur business. About 1840, fashion in Europe decreed that beaver hats were no longer stylish, and time was needed to develop other uses for the beautiful furs of North America. Bateaux piled with furs lined the docks of Montreal, Quebec, and other St. Lawrence port cities. As word drifted back up the lakes, fur-laden canoes no longer shot the rapids at Sault Ste. Marie during spring and summer, and far back into the wilderness there was hunger and disappointment and dismay.

A third cause of change—this a good one for the area—was the discovery, in the 1840's, of minerals on the shores of Lake Superior. The state of Michigan had appointed Dr. Douglass Houghton, a

well-known young geologist, to explore the northern shore of upper
Michigan. With a few helpers, Houghton sailed along near the shore
of Lake Superior; he made five landings, each time staying for
careful tests and studies. He sank the first salt well in the area, a
forerunner of a great chemical industry. He found a little iron. And
he confirmed the many Indian legends when he discovered copper
on the Keweenaw Peninsula. This copper, in the purest form known,
was lying on the ground, left by the retreating glaciers that had
scooped out the lake basins.

Houghton's official report was cautious; he warned that moving
even surface copper down to where industries were located would
take considerable capital. But at that time men were not in a mood
for caution. It was a time of adventure: men had courage, not
caution. Scores hurried north expecting to wrest fortune from the
ground with their bare hands. Most of them failed. Others, who
waited to raise capital and who had the necessary knowledge, suc-
ceeded. Young Dr. Houghton was drowned in a storm in Lake
Superior; his wisdom might have helped many, for he was gener-
ous with his knowledge.

But as always, someone else took up needed work. William
Burt was a deputy surveyor under Dr. Houghton; he had taught
himself surveying as had many other Americans—George Washington and Andrew Jackson, for instance. Burt had an inventive
mind; he had made the first attempt at a typewriter and had invented a solar compass which could determine location by sun,
instead of magnetic force.

On a late summer day in 1844, Burt and his helpers were
surveying in northern Michigan, a few miles from where the city of
Marquette was built later. The day was cloudy, a disappointment
because the solar compass could not be used. Suddenly the magnetic
needle began to dance.

"You'll have to spread out, boys," Burt called, "and find out what makes the trouble." They found croppings of iron in several places.

"Hard luck," Burt said. "Maybe tomorrow the sun will shine and we can use the solar compass." He mentioned iron in his report, but the item was not noticed. No one was interested in iron.

Some time later Philo Everet of Jackson, Michigan, came north to search for silver which he had heard was on the peninsula. Word of discoveries traveled fast even without radio or television; often reports were exaggerated, but Everet cared enough to go and search for himself. At Sault Ste. Marie he hired an Indian guide and while buying supplies, chanced to hear of Burt's discovery.

"Can you show me where iron is?" he asked his guide.

"Yes, I can. But that black stuff is no good."

"Well, I'd like to see it, anyway," Everet answered.

He saw—and quickly went back to Jackson, formed a company, raised capital, and got that iron into use. Everet was one of the few who in that year saw a future for iron; he soon had a long trail of followers.

Getting iron out and moving it down nearer coal mines where it could be reduced to useful form, proved to be a major problem. As raw ore it was bulky. And Lake Superior was as remote from the other lakes as Lake Ontario once had been. Men were not thinking about a through waterway; they simply wanted to get ore down. The one ship which had been built on Lake Superior was soon swamped with orders for transport. Barges, hurriedly built, were good enough in fine weather, but in a storm were apt to overturn— men and ore going to the bottom of a very deep, cold lake.

Then there was the problem of getting ore to a landing and then onto a ship or barge. Some companies dragged the ore to shore by cart in summer, by sled in winter. Ore itself was heavy and bulky. It could be melted into ingots at the mine or by the shore —but it could not be loaded into a birchbark canoe. And there was that mile at Sault Ste. Marie where iron must be carried or carted—a slow, expensive operation.

As the mining business grew, word of jobs spread and more families came north, increasing the congestion and confusion at the village by the rapids. A prosperous portage business grew fast. Men in the village lucky enough to have carts made "good money." Boys carried boxes or valises for a dime—that seemed like wealth. The village had never dreamed of such prosperity.

Seldon McKnight was the first villager to develop a real portage business. He not only had a cart, but also an old gray horse. The next year he risked getting several carts and horses and had more business than he could handle. So he built a railroad along the main street—now Portage Street—with wooden rails covered with iron strips to withstand the hard usage he expected. Small wooden carts, horse-drawn, moved through the village hauling iron ore, copper, and grain going down; machinery and general cargo going up. McKnight charged five cents a hundred pounds, with extra charge if cargo had to be put in his new warehouse to wait its turn for a ship. That warehouse was a good idea—and profitable, too.

McKnight's scheme for a railroad portage would not have suited the needs on the Niagara Peninsula a generation earlier— even if it had been thought of at that time. At the Niagara Peninsula the more than three-hundred-foot drop needed oxen to pull carts up or ease loads down. At the St. Marys rapids the fall was only twenty-one feet to the mile—a drop hardly noticed in a mile of village street. Yet the force of Lake Superior waters flowing down, the size and placement of rocks in the rapids, made the one mile an impossible barrier to transportation of the new cargoes.

Villagers were prosperous and happy as never before. Shippers and travelers fretted at delays and expense, but no one suggested a remedy except more portage, as confusion grew worse and piled-up cargoes mounted higher.

One unexpected result was the beginning of a lively tourist business; shippers and families en route must be housed and fed as they waited. And they had time to see the rare beauty of the rapids and the forests. Many wrote letters and sent them back by steamer to Detroit. One letter said: "You should come and see this place and 'shoot the rapids'—an adventurous sport that the Indians do well."

Some day, with this kind of publicity, Sault Ste. Marie would not seem as far away as the moon.

CHAPTER 8

Sault Ste. Marie

Among the many who heard of the rapids during the early 1850's and came to see the place for themselves was young Charles Harvey of New England. Harvey had left his native Connecticut and gone to Vermont, where he got a job with the E. and T. Fairbanks Company selling platform scales. Like many other easterners, they were interested in the West; so they sent Charles Harvey to sell scales in lower Michigan.

All went well until Harvey was taken ill with typhoid fever—a disease that, along with cholera, was a deadly foe at that time. If one lived through typhoid, as Harvey did, there was still a long, slow convalescence to endure. He had heard about the fine air "up north," so he decided to visit the Lake Superior country, recover his health and, he hoped, sell some scales at the same time.

Sault Ste. Marie was looking its best when Harvey walked away from the S. S. *Northern*, docked at the foot of the rapids, and set out to find a ship to take him to Lake Superior. The village of five hundred people was crowded with travelers. Local men and boys rushed about, helping unload cargoes, load portage cars, carts, and wheelbarrows.

"Carry your bag, Mister?" a boy yelled and grabbed Harvey's valise before the question was answered.

Harvey found he was lucky to get passage on a ship that would sail west as soon as cargo was loaded. He used the few days of waiting to make acquaintances and to watch portage. When he returned in late August, he was feeling well and was much pleased with his selling record.

But what interested him even more than health or business was the talk he had heard about need for a canal with locks to bypass the mile of rapids. Men in the iron ore business up north complained bitterly about delays at Sault Ste. Marie. Large sources of coal had been located below the lower lakes; iron ore should be brought to the coal, men told Harvey. Factories and mills in growing cities along the southern lake shores clamored for ore; they could use any amount of it! And here it lay—piles of it—awaiting ships.

Harvey knew that in 1851 the legislature of Michigan had considered a bill about a canal. It was a petition asking the federal government for half a million dollars to build a canal with locks by the rapids. Prosperous portage people had worked hard against the bill.

"We don't need an expensive canal," they said. "We get the cargo moved."

"Send ships through by canal and our village people will starve!"

They lobbied so successfully that the bill failed to pass.

Then that August of 1852, just when Harvey chanced to be passing through the village, word came that the United States congress had set aside land—not money, but three-quarters of a million acres of public land—to be sold to the people. The money from this sale was to be used to construct a canal and locks at the St. Marys rapids. The bill carried definite specifications about the project: it was to be at least 100 feet wide, and 12 feet deep, with two lock chambers, tandem style, each chamber 250 feet long and 60 feet wide with a total lift and lower power of 20 feet. The bill required that work begin before the end of three years and be completed by ten. A strip of land, paralleling the rapids and 400 feet wide, was allotted for this use.

Harvey's imagination was stirred; he determined to build that canal! He had already written to the Fairbanks brothers about the great need for such a waterway. Now he studied that four-hundred-foot strip; he made sketches and figured finances. Time was needed to sell land; meanwhile, acres would not buy tools nor pay contractors and workmen. Men with money must be interested; a company must be formed to advance cash and start the work while the land was being sold. Like Merritt before him, Harvey knew that he must go east at once and raise capital.

The Fairbanks brothers and others were immediately responsive; they set about raising money and forming a company. Harvey hunted up L. L. Nichols, an engineer who had worked on the Erie Canal, and the two men went to Sault Ste. Marie to make a careful survey before winter put a stop to shipping. While Nichols measured and figured, Harvey borrowed a canoe and went down the St. Marys River looking for stone which could be used to line the locks. Nichols had told him that wood in the Welland locks had had to be replaced in ten years—Harvey meant his locks to be durable.

After the turn of the year Harvey went to Lansing to meet and talk with members of the state legislature—he was the only really informed man there. But he was not the only interested visitor; portage people from the village were there in full force, ready to tell every legislator why a canal should not be built. It was really confusing.

Then to everyone's amazement, Harvey himself added to the tumult by proposing that the canal and locks should be even larger than congress required! Why should a man who favored the canal raise *any* objection? The portage people stirred up enough trouble.

"You talk like a portage man," one puzzled senator exclaimed. "You want locks *three* hundred and fifty feet long?" Harvey nodded. "There'll never be a ship on the lakes long enough to need such a lock! You should know that, young man."

"I predict that within twenty-five years you'll see big ships going through the Sault," Harvey said, boldly. "And they'll carry more tonnage than goes through the Straits of Mackinac." The legislators laughed, thinking that Harvey was making a joke.

But Charles Harvey had a convincing way. The bill—with the longer locks—was passed. It had one other change, hardly noticed at the moment; the time allowed for construction was slyly changed from ten years to two—two years, a mere twenty-four months, to finance, get under way, and complete construction of a mile of canal with two stone-lined locks and proper gates—far away from markets, labor, and supplies. Portage men who had had that new section inserted went home in fine spirits. No company could do that job in two years. The project was bound to fail, and they would do business as usual.

Harvey hid his shock and accepted the challenge.

With a companion, he went north to select land to be set aside for the sale. Three quarters of a million acres seemed vast wealth. Actually, the value of the land was not known; much sold for twenty-five cents an acre; seventy-five cents was a high price. The value varied, too. Harvey's earlier studies enabled him to make wise selections that benefited the company forming in the east. In the middle of winter he got himself to Sault Ste. Marie and registered plots of land in lower and upper Michigan, and he indicated which he wished sold first.

Meanwhile money was raised in the east and sent to Harvey at Detroit. He was made general manager and began buying tools and materials and hiring men. Harvey was then twenty-four years old, and like Hamilton Merritt, was well equipped with energy, imagination, and faith in himself.

It was in Detroit as spring came and he was spending the $50,000 sent to him, that the full force of the two-year clause overwhelmed him. He bought hurriedly: shovels, pickaxes, wheelbarrows, a few mules—not many were obtainable; the work on this project, as on the Erie and the Welland, must be done by manpower. He bought food and hired a ship and all the men he could persuade to go with him. On the voyage north he explained plans for each man's work so clearly that when the ship docked at the foot of the rapids, everyone knew exactly what he was expected to do— and did it. Long cabins, bunkhouses, Harvey called them, were built for housing the work force, also a cookhouse. A hot supper was served at the end of the second day, and every man had bedding and a place to sleep.

Early the next morning, Harvey led a march to the line he had stretched and joined in the ceremony of "first digging." When Harvey shouted, "Digging begins!" work began to overcome a formidable barrier in a waterway from Lake Superior ports to the sea. If he could succeed—again the thought of that two-year requirement struck him like a blow. Could he possibly do it? Not by standing there dreaming! He glanced at the men, tossing earth, and strode off to his own tasks.

Difficulties turned up almost at once, the first being mosquitoes.

The pests came in clouds. Men deserted, chancing walking back to Detroit rather than staying. Harvey sent advertisements to port cities to attract newly arrived immigrants, but many men hesitated to go so far into a distant wilderness. Before the canal was finished, Harvey was advertising in papers in a dozen foreign cities. Men from Germany, Ireland, Scotland, Sweden, Finland, and other countries were working on the job. It was this mixture of languages that brought about the changed spelling of the word Sault to the phonetic spelling, Soo. This had been a place of many names; now no one seems surprised that the cities by the rapids keep the French Sault Ste. Marie; the river uses the English words St. Marys, and the area has the generally accepted nickname, the Soo.

Another difficulty was the discovery that some of the digging area was solid rock; it had to be blasted. The nearest dynamite was in Delaware; the nearest point for sending a telegraph message, Detroit. This was the time when each railroad company laid its tracks with its own gauge; rails were four to six feet apart, and it was not possible to ship freight or passengers right through. At the end of each road there was a grand change. This, of course, was before convenience of shippers and travelers was considered important, and it made a great difference—especially to a general manager awaiting goods at the Soo.

Health was another problem in that far-off place. Harvey met this by action, not mere sympathy. On a small island he had a comfortable little cabin built as a hospital, and he engaged a doctor and a nurse. The men were charged twenty-five cents a month from their wages, and the company paid the remaining costs. This was a novel idea that created good will and saved lives.

Work went on through the winter. Bonfires flamed, and if a man showed signs of frostbite, he was ordered to take time out and warm himself. Harvey hovered by the mile-long ditch, doing his own work of accounting, letter writing, and planning at night.

Building the locks began in the spring of 1854. Some walls were
of natural rock; other walls were built of stone brought from
Drummond Island, down the river.

With the coming of good weather, the state of Michigan sent
Captain Canfield, the army engineer who had made the original
survey, to inspect the work, and the company in the east sent a
committee to see that their money was being wisely spent.

"You can't possibly finish in time," the visitors agreed. Harvey
found them a drain on time and faith when he had none to spare.
Money was running short, too. The public land sold slowly; it
was a difficult period.

The army map showed a sand bar, west of the head of the
canal, but the bar proved to be rock, solid rock—and it must be

moved. Harvey contrived a steam gravity punch that let down a huge timber with force that shattered off rock, a device that had half the rock moved by the time dynamite arrived. Cholera, a bitter winter—nothing stopped the work.

In April of 1855 the lock walls were finished, the wooden gates were in place, the canal banks smoothed. There remained only to dig the short, final section at the west end of the canal and let the waters of Lake Superior into the new connecting link. Before this digging began, there must be a cofferdam built to hold back the flow of water while the final digging was done. This cofferdam was not Harvey's responsibility; Captain Canfield had made the design, and the dam was partly finished when he suddenly died. His assistants finished as best they knew; there was no time to wait for another engineer. In a final test the cofferdam failed to hold; Harvey dared not risk men's lives by having them dig behind that uncertain protection.

This was a moment when courage all but failed him. He paced back and forth by the handsome locks—dry as dust, of course. He studied the short section of land yet to be removed, fighting despair. Then, suddenly, he turned and shouted to the nearest man.

"There's a ship at the foot of the rapids! *Run!* Buy all the sailcloth the captain will sell you!"

"Sailcloth!" The man stared.

"Yes, sailcloth. Buy all the captain will sell you!"

Soon a bolt of heavy sailcloth was unrolled upon the ground near the unfinished portion of the canal. Harvey did not explain. He did not dare risk laughter and lack of faith—not now. Soon he had them making a wide hem along one side, attaching floats to the parallel edge.

"Now fill the hem with gravel," he ordered. "Shake it in . . . maybe we'd better lay the gravel on first and turn the hem over it . . . ."

"Bring up canoes, you, there! Take that end and climb in . . . careful now!" Two men in each canoe dragged that weighted sailcloth out over the water to an island. For a breathless moment they waited—then the gravel-weighted edge sank slowly out of sight. Floats held the upper edge on the surface. That crude improvised dam held.

A gang of men began making another strip to place above the first; others tossed rock and gravel to hold the hem down. Some set flares. All other workers began digging at that strip of land— digging that would continue day and night until the opening was complete.

On the 19th of April, 1855, Harvey cautiously loosened the south edge of his sailcloth dam and let a little water trickle through. He moved it further, and water trickled into the west lock.

"Close the lower gates," he called. "We'll let the water in."

Word spread around the village, and men, women, and children ran to see the opening of the canal. Awed, they watched as the trickle became a stream that backed up against the gate—and the gate held. Cautiously the gates were opened; the canal began to fill—the job was finished, and in twenty-two and a half months. Of course lights must be set, walks laid, a dozen minor tasks completed before the official opening; but there was ample time.

The S.S. *Illinois* locked through the new canal on June 28th, 1855, the honor of being "first up" going to Captain John Wilson. For days vessels had been jockeying below the canal entrance for this distinction. Every part of the new operation went smoothly— the turning gates, the inflowing water raising the ship, the smooth exit at the western end. The whole process took about twenty minutes, *minutes*, not days, as with portage. Many villagers neglected dinner and stayed to watch the S.S. *Baltimore* come down with a load of copper; the reverse process was equally successful.

On that day of rejoicing no one used the words "Great Lakes-

St. Lawrence Seaway" because at that moment in the nineteenth century men were not thinking of a long waterway; the urgent need was to get metals down to cities on the lower lakes, surplus grain to mills, and people with their goods and supplies to the northwest. But now that the two greatest natural barriers to continuous navigation—Niagara Falls and the rapids at the Soo—were successfully bypassed, men's vision would lengthen and their ambitions and faith would grow.

CHAPTER 9

Ships and Cities

WHILE Houghton, Burt, Everet, and others were finding vast resources in northern Michigan, more and more people came from Europe to ports in the United States and Canada. The Erie Canal carried hundreds on west; the Welland Canal was so much used that it soon proved to be too small; its wooden locks wore down, too, and had to be replaced. In 1843 the Canadian government bought this canal from the original company, paid the investors their capital investment with interest, and then built a larger canal with fewer locks.

Some canals along the St. Lawrence River were widened and deepened, too. By 1860, five years after the canal at the Soo was opened, a few small ships were taking cargo across the ocean without transshipping. Such commerce was limited, of course, by the size of the smallest canal on the river. Intercity shipping was more profitable and was the major part of all lake commerce.

Political events in the United States and in Canada between the years 1854 and 1867 tended to increase contacts between the two nations and to add to the prosperity of both. Canada had changed her monetary system from pounds to dollars; the value of the United States and the Canadian dollars was never identical but the difference was slight, and the common name seemed to make computations simpler in business and in travel. In 1854 the two countries signed a Reciprocity Treaty by which the natural products of each country were admitted to the other interchangeably without duty. By this treaty, too, United States fishermen were allowed to fish along the Maritime Provinces, Canadians were given the right to use Lake Michigan waters, and Americans, the right to use the St. Lawrence River and its canals. These courtesies, especially the use of the river, were important steps toward the later co-operation in the building of a seaway. After this treaty, trade flowed briskly and both nations prospered.

This was a time of rapid growth of railroads; they seem always to have grown and prospered during periods of growth of lake shipping. As a war measure, President Lincoln decreed that all railroads should use George Stephenson's track gauge as standard— four feet, eight and one-half inches between rails. Railroad companies accepted his decision, and as fast as standard tracks could be laid, railroad travel was improved. This resulted in more transport from the hinterlands to lake ports and aided business.

Growing interchange between the two countries caused a demand for a bridge near Montreal. The Prince of Wales came over to lay the final stone in the handsome bridge named Victoria to honor the queen. This bridge benefited not only Canada but New York and New England areas. Its construction is so sound that seaway engineers have accepted it. Modern lifts, approaches, and traffic lights provide for uninterrupted flow of traffic.

During the war between the states England supported the South—she needed cotton for her mills. This fact startled Canadians; suppose the United States should turn upon Canada? Could scattered provinces meet such attack? This question was an important factor in a decision to join together and form the Dominion of Canada—a united nation spread over the entire upper portion of North America. The once tiny trading village of Bytown, on the Ottawa River, became the capital of the new Dominion and was called Ottawa. Stately buildings were erected where once Indians, Black Robes, and traders had been the only travelers. The birthday of this new political union was July 1, 1867, the same week as its neighbor's birthday, July 4th, ninety-one years earlier.

After the war the United States began widening and straightening the St. Marys River—a task that continues to this day, for as fast as improvements are made, larger vessels demand better channels. In 1876 the United States began building a second lock at the Soo; this Weitzel Lock was 515 feet long, a size that was expected to be adequate for all time. But even as it was opened in 1881, new ships already challenged that idea!

Changing types of craft on the lakes told the tale of growing water transport. Durham boats replaced birchbark canoes; sailing vessels outmoded Durhams; steamers, though more costly to build and operate, challenged sailing ships.

Back in 1809, two years after Robert Fulton took the steamer *Clermont* up the Hudson, an enterprising Canadian firm built the S.S. *Accommodation*, a steamer with a six horsepower engine and side paddles that churned water into glistening foam. The river banks at Montreal were crowded on the Wednesday afternoon when the *Accommodation* departed for Quebec City. She arrived at Quebec Saturday morning—both nights, of course, were spent lying at anchor, for there were as yet no such safety aids as lights on land or steamer. The return voyage was less glorious, because the valiant little engine could not compete with the river's swift current near the journey's end; ox teams dragged the steamer to her dock at Montreal.

S.S. *Walk-in-the-Water* was the first steamer on the Great Lakes. Built in 1818, in Niagara River near Lake Erie, she was followed by a long series of side-wheelers. These were expensive to build and operate; like steamers on the Ohio and Mississippi rivers, they were luxurious. They had paneled lounges and wide, carpeted stairways; meals with many courses were served. But they had disadvantages, too, besides cost. There were long delays while a steamer took on incredible amounts of firewood which, later, would shower the deck with hot cinders. But in spite of annoyances, steamers got the main passenger service from Buffalo up the lakes; only thrifty immigrants used sailing ships.

St. Lawrence canals were not suited to large side-wheelers, and until the late 1840's no steamer risked the rapids. They were considered impassable, an idea that was proved wrong by the S.S. *Ontario*. This steamer was built for travel on Lake Ontario, but she proved to be so fast that a company wanted her for trips between Montreal and Quebec. But how to get her down? She could not use the small canals; no such vessel had dared the rapids. Determined men called in Old Jock and Old Pete, the best Indian pilots on the river, and put the problem up to them.

"Give you each a thousand dollars if you get her safely to Montreal," company men told the pilots. The Indians accepted, and company men worried. The story of the Indians' method was later told by a river man named Johnson, who had heard it from Old Jock:

"A crib some forty feet square was built with floats ten feet apart and with wooden stakes projecting downward from every space between squares. When this odd-looking thing was ready,

watchers were hurried down the river—one at the head, one at the
foot of each rapids, and several high in trees in between. The crib
was towed to the head of the most western of the rapids—the Galop
—and given to the current. Each keen-eyed Indian watched as the
current swirled the crib down the river. At Montreal the crib was
turned over, and it was seen that not one of the stakes was broken—
proof that water was deep enough for the *Ontario* to go through.

"Upriver the whole group of Indians boarded the steamer, and
each man piloted her through the section that he had watched."
The only person aboard who was not an Indian was the engineer,

and the grateful company gave him a thousand dollars, too.

This feat led toward tourist travel on the rapids, so popular that in time a special steamer, the *Rapids Prince*, was built for this trade. Passengers left palatial steamers at Prescott and on the small *Rapids Prince* took the thrilling day's journey to Montreal that only the stouthearted could really enjoy. The captain and an Indian pilot stood on the bridge sternly watching white foam and dark rocks. No passenger would dare speak to them.

"Hi Yi!" The Indian shouted the age-old cry of danger; the helmsman swiftly whirled the wheel—just in time! Often the hull scraped a rock, and the jar tossed passengers sprawling on the deck. Such incidents made wonderful tales to recount at home—in Virginia or Indiana—but were hard on the steamer. Another ship, the *Prince Albert*, was built as an alternate. This tourist trade continued until about 1952. Then, because both steamers needed expensive repairs at a time when the rapids were about to vanish before the new seaway, the service was discontinued.

During the later part of the nineteenth century vacationers spread over the entire Great Lakes area. People were prosperous; annual vacations were more common. The Thousand Islands, one of the most picturesque sections of the long waterway, suddenly became fashionable. The migrating Loyalists had discovered the charm of this region decades earlier; many a family had bought an island and built a home on one side and a business, usually a shipyard, on the other. When tourists arrived, a few ornate hotels were built "to take boarders." Families who came back each year bought an island—a small, round, wooded gem with a cottage, a dock, a rowboat, and perhaps a "naphtha launch." So outfitted, a family felt like royalty. Such use of river islands is rare in the world, as water levels in most rivers are subject to sudden change—the Mississippi, for instance, varies seventy feet according to flood or dry season. The St. Lawrence varies less than ten feet, sometimes less than half that amount. The five lakes above, and especially the very deep Ontario, act as reservoirs holding the water level quite steady.

Passengers aboard steamers saw the enchanting islands, the cottages with wide porches, swimmers idling on the docks, and spread the fame of the area. The water was chilly, but women and girls were well protected in garments of navy blue woolen serge, full bloomers and skirts, long-sleeved blouses with lined sailor collars, and long black stockings. Men and boys were rather less burdened but still well protected. Passengers and islanders waved cordially—all was gay and agreeable.

Of course tourist trade, while profitable, was only froth; the real business on the lakes was shipping bulk and general cargo. There was a sense of immediacy about lake shipping; ore and grain must be got down, and coal and merchandise moved up before ice closed ports and channels. When the great Mesabi iron range was discovered in the late 1880's, this sense of hurry increased. Lake cities "down below" wanted iron. Other industries were overlooked in the stampede to beat the winter with rich ore.

Lake towns and cities developed industries and grew rapidly. Already, in the latter part of the nineteenth century, it had become impossible to recount achievements in the tale of one man as it was with early explorers, or even as late as with Merritt and Harvey. Hundreds of men made cities, sailed ships, excavated ore and raised grain. The history of lake commerce was written by industries, by ports; thousands of people promoted growth on the lakes, thousands earned good livings on its shores.

Kingston, on Lake Ontario, was a shipbuilding center from its earliest days. Later it stored grain for transshipping; huge elevators rose higher and higher as prairie harvests grew. Toronto, in addition to its shipyards and grain storage, developed what became a world-wide business in seeds and nursery goods, along

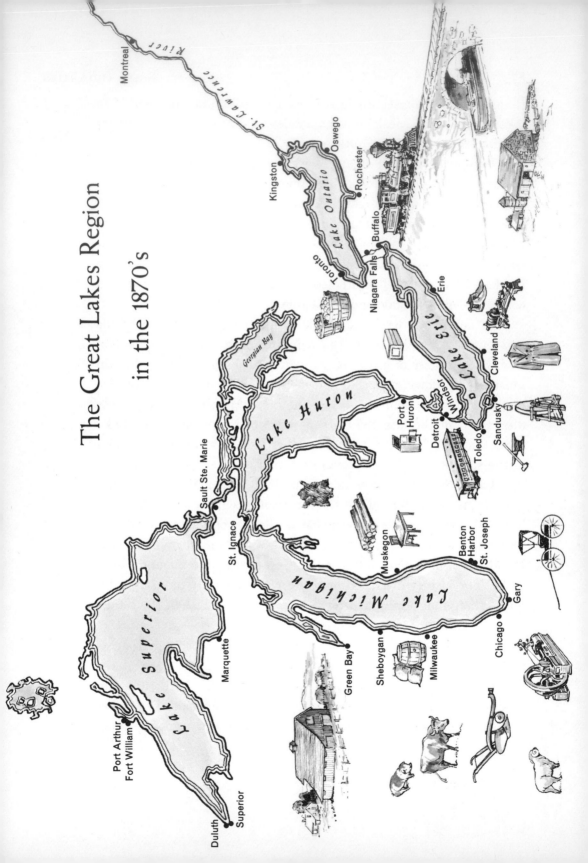

The Great Lakes Region

in the 1870's

St. Lawrence River

Montreal

Kingston

Oswego

Rochester

Lake Ontario

Toronto

Buffalo

Niagara Falls

Erie

Georgian Bay

Lake Erie

Cleveland

Lake Huron

Windsor

Sandusky

Port Huron

Detroit

Toledo

Sault Ste. Marie

St. Ignace

Muskegon

Benton Harbor

St. Joseph

Lake Superior

Marquette

Gary

Green Bay

Sheboygan

Chicago

Milwaukee

Port Arthur

Fort William

Lake Michigan

Duluth

Superior

with a variety of other industries. Hamilton shipped threshing machines and fine fruits: plums, peaches, apples, and other fruits grown on the fertile peninsula.

On the southern shore of Lake Ontario, Rochester and Oswego had shipyards, grain storage, and flour mills; and Rochester's German citizens used climate and soil resources so well in floriculture that Rochester earned the name "The Flower City."

On Lake Erie, Buffalo—with railroads and the Erie Canal at her door—became an important grain center, transshipping over the world. She pioneered in shipping coal north in grain boats—a use of the return voyage that was adopted by other port cities. Before the turn of the century her other industries were varied: soap, starch, scales, oil, wallpaper, fertilizer, and, later, iron parts for bridges and for farm and mill machinery.

Cleveland made clothing, shoes, machinery, and engines. But farsighted businessmen saw that a great future lay in steel. By 1885 one steel mill employed a thousand men—and there were, by then, many mills. Toledo, Sandusky, Erie—all these grew rapidly and prospered; with lake shipping in front and railroads leading back, they could ship their products near and far.

Detroit and Windsor, just across from each other on the Detroit River, were natural shipping ports. Their people saw ore boats lengthen out, engine at the stern, pilothouse at the bow. They saw ore boats, grain boats, oil boats; the word "boat" became accepted for a laker. An ocean-going vessel is of course a ship, but a laker may properly be called a boat.

Detroit is said to be the first city with a plant using the Bessemer method for making steel, but she did not specialize in steel as some other cities did. By 1870 Detroit was making sleeping cars and refrigerator cars, and soon afterwards, drugs, clothing, hardware, wooden goods, and, later, automobiles. Men flocked to Detroit for jobs.

This city was a pioneer in providing recreation for its people. In 1879 the city bought Belle Isle, a beautiful wooded island a few miles up the river, and turned it into a handsome public park. A day's excursion by steamer up to the island was a joy shared by tourists and Detroiters alike. While on this island many people got their first sight of the long lakers and their first knowledge of the great quantity of lake shipping.

Lake Huron had few industrial towns at this time, but every river and stream sent logs down to the lake, logs that were gathered into rafts for towing or loaded on barges or sailing ships. Yellow pine from Lake Huron forests, especially on the Michigan side, often crowded the ore-boat traffic going downriver to the lower lakes or around into Lake Michigan.

Lake Michigan, with rich farm lands west and south, had many prosperous cities—Escanaba, Sheboygan, Milwaukee, Chicago, St. Joseph, Muskegon, and others. Most of these had industries similar to those along Lake Erie, with farm machinery and other farm needs taking a lead.

Chicago, with its fortunate location, became such a railroad center that it was called the Hub City, its tracks radiating out like spokes to far hinterlands. The Illinois and Michigan canal was built, and wagon roads were laid out earlier than in some places. As settlers opened up the rich Mississippi Valley, farm products naturally came to Chicago and nearby cities for sale or for shipping further.

Steel mills grew so fast that new cities such as Gary and Indiana Harbor grew up, employing thousands; in Chicago, plants were built for meat packing and for making farm machinery and general merchandise. All this, along with agricultural products which flowed to the city, spurred the development of rail, water, and highway transport. Railroads reached out where cheaper water transport did not go. Vessels of all sorts jammed the little Chicago River; shipping on the lakes was lively and profitable, but shipping overseas, while technically possible, was too limited by the shallow canals along the St. Lawrence to be significant in the general movement of goods. Perhaps that was just as well, many thought, for even with the new breakwater built by the federal government, the port was often too crowded.

Along the shores of Lake Superior, Port Arthur and Fort William, Duluth and Superior, shipped grain and some metal; Marquette, iron and copper. Canada's Sault Ste. Marie made steel and had one of the early paper mills.

Shipping in this whole area changed as if by magic with the finding of Mesabi iron; there was enough iron in Minnesota to last a hundred years—two hundred years—who could tell how much there was? Ships were made longer, loading and unloading were done faster by new machinery. The new industries craved iron, begged for steel—get it down fast! was the constant cry. Boats did not bother with return cargo; they raced back north, high in the water, ready for more of this rich ore.

Fortunately, at Marquette—an iron shipping port too—there was a man who had had long experience in shipping and who had developed methods of loading cargo faster. Peter White was one of several men whose genius helped lake shipping. His family had moved from Troy, New York, to Green Bay, Wisconsin, when he was a boy of nine. In Green Bay he heard tales of the "upper country"—around Lake Superior. When he was fifteen he ran away, got a job with a mining company near Lake Superior and, with many others, walked there, carrying mine machinery on his back. In spite of cold, ice, and mosquitoes, Peter stayed on and grew up with that country. Through the inspiration of Peter White, excellent iron furnaces were built on the Marquette Peninsula so that iron ore could be reduced into pig iron before shipping. He also was a leader in expediting the loading and unloading of ore boats, by installing machinery instead of using man power. His block and tackle with a big basket scoop at the end of a chain lifted iron from pier to dock so fast—compared with men and wheelbarrows—that 400 tons could be loaded in a little over two days. This simple contrivance was the forerunner of the overhead traveling cranes, giant chutes, and other machinery that makes possible loading or unloading thousand of tons in four hours.

On the fiftieth anniversary of the opening of Michigan's first canal and locks at the Soo, Peter White was invited, along with others, to celebrate the occasion, to see the new locks, and to make a speech. In part he said:

"A long water haul is so enormously cheaper than a long rail haul that the ability to ship large cargoes direct from Lake Superior ports, twelve hundred, thirteen hundred miles, or even across the seas, has transformed the United States and changed her position among nations."

He told of grain going to Liverpool, of copper—potential electric wires, making life easier and cheaper for all mankind. He spoke of the new Mesabi iron, going to America and to many other nations in the form of machinery, rails, guns, hammers, reapers, bridges. His imagination saw that this flow of goods was outmoding canals and locks once thought large enough for all time. He named men who had a share in making this prosperity possible. He ended:

"These men have proved that peace is greater than war and that commerce is the handmaiden of peace."

CHAPTER 10

A Seaway—For and Against

A NEW era in lake shipping began when the first cargo of Mesabi iron ore came down from Lake Superior in 1892. The quality was so good, the quantity so great, certainly too much for North Americans alone—why not ship oversea? The waterway was continuous to the ocean; many people failed to understand that it was not therefore navigable for ore boats.

Of the natural barriers on the 2342-mile length of the Great Lakes–St. Lawrence waterway—rapids at the Soo, Niagara Falls, and several stretches of rapids on the river—the Soo in the nineties was the best equipped to serve the lakers. The United States had built the Weitzel Lock, opened in 1881, 515 feet long and 17 feet deep. Canada had built a lock along the north shore in 1895, the

An ore carrier of the United States Steel Corporation passing through a lock at Sault Ste. Marie, laden with iron ore and bound for the steel mills at South Chicago or Gary.

lock 900 feet long and at that time 22 feet deep (at the present lower lake levels it is now 16.8 feet deep). In 1896, the United States opened the Poe Lock, 704 feet long and then 22 feet deep (now 16.6); in 1914, the Davis Lock, 1350 feet long and then 24½ feet deep (now, 23.1); in 1919, the Sabin Lock, a twin of the Davis Lock was opened. These locks bear the names of United States army engineers who worked in the area. In 1943, the MacArthur Lock, 800 feet long, 80 feet wide and 31 feet deep over the sills at present water levels, was opened and named for Douglas MacArthur, the famous general of World War II and the Korean War. This lock replaced the Weitzel Lock. The Poe Lock is to be replaced with a new lock to accommodate seaway traffic.

The locks of the third Welland Canal, opened in 1887, were 14 feet deep, matching the canals along the St. Lawrence. This limited a vessel to a draught of 12½ feet; lock lengths were usually about 270 feet, too short for the profitable new lakers. Most lake commerce continued to be between cities on the four upper lakes. Beyond, grain or ore must be transshipped, a costly process.

By 1895, the bottlenecks below Lake Erie were such a handicap that Canada and the United States appointed a commission of engineers and prominent citizens, three from each country, to study and report on the advisability of constructing a deep channel from the Great Lakes to the Atlantic Ocean. This was the first of several commissions appointed by the United States and Canada during the next sixty years. Each made some contribution; each by discussion and publicity helped the public understand the growing need for a navigable outlet to the sea by way of the Great Lakes and the St. Lawrence River.

One of the most experienced men on this first International Commission was Thomas C. Keefer, a Canadian civil engineer. He was born four years before the Erie Canal opened; when he was eighteen, he served as a maintenance engineer of that canal. He was the chief engineer in the building of the famous log chutes on the Ottawa River, and he knew the St. Lawrence River well. To him the problem before the commission was simple: build bigger and better canals and locks. He had been writing and talking about such construction since before the war between the states and the formation of the Dominion. He believed that the interior of North America could become a seaport for the world; he may have been the first to use that phrase.

The plan he proposed was, in essence, the plan actually carried out sixty years later, but many people had to be convinced of the need before any such work could be done. There was much talk of waterways, and many plans, some of them fantastic, were proposed.

An example was the plan of Narcisse Cantin.

Narcisse was the son of a French-Canadian shipbuilder; the family lived in the town of St. Joseph on the east shore of Lake Huron. He was an unusual lad; at seventeen a successful cattle dealer and a sparring partner of the famous prize fighter, John L. Sullivan. About the time Mesabi ore was discovered, Narcisse moved to Buffalo, where he had an excellent chance to see firsthand how much the Welland and Erie canals had done for business. His thoughts went back to his own quiet home town—a forty-to fifty-mile-long canal dug across country to Lake Erie would save miles of water travel . . . Better still, a new canal on the peninsula would save even more mileage to Lake Ontario and beyond. He went home, talked canals, spent his own money to build up St. Joseph so it would be ready for the boom these canals would bring . . . His dream failed. Cantin lost everything and had to start over. But his daring, his faith in canals, never failed. Men like him, some with success, some with failure at the moment, kept public interest in water transport growing.

In the twentieth century, with the progress of the industrial age, people talked and thought more of waterways. The Suez Canal, opened in 1869, had connected the Red and Mediterranean seas. Talk of a canal on the Isthmus of Panama was revived; that project had been started but had been stopped by yellow fever. After yellow fever was conquered, the Panama Canal was built by the United States. It was opened in 1914, in time to prove its great value during World War I. This feat encouraged both the United States and Canada and stimulated interest in improving navigation on the St. Lawrence River.

In 1900, one of the commissions, a group of engineers appointed by the United States senate, recommended to the president that the United States build a canal of her own, 21 feet deep, and on the American side of the Long Sault Rapids. This definite proposal led the United States to ask Canada to appoint what was called the International Waterways Commission with three members from each country. The commission studied and reported on such important matters as Niagara power, St. Lawrence power, water levels in the lakes, diversion of water for the Chicago Drainage Canal, channels in the St. Marys River, boundary water problems, and many other matters brought to joint consideration for the first time.

Largely as a result of these studies, a Boundary Waters Treaty was entered into in 1909, and an International Joint Commission was appointed and made a part of the treaty. This commission has continued through the intervening years. It seemed for a time that action on seaway improvements would result. But soon World War I was both a reason and an excuse for dropping the whole matter.

With great foresight and courage Congressman Bertrand H. Snell of Potsdam, New York, introduced a bill in the United States congress, April 24, 1917, on the subject of seaway-power development. The bill would authorize the secretary of war to make surveys and collect data with a view of creating with Canada a navigable seaway "for ocean-going ships . . . in or paralleling the St. Lawrence River . . . to get an approximate estimate of costs and of the amount of power, if any, that would be incident thereto . . ." The congressman made an impassioned speech for such a seaway, the first on this subject heard on the floor of congress.

There was a great show of public interest. Competent staffs went to work; scores of meetings were held; testimony, mostly favorable, was taken for study. But the bill died in the committee.

In 1924, President Coolidge appointed a United States Committee with Secretary of Commerce Herbert Hoover chairman—all seemed going well for speedy construction.

But opposition, long smoldering, flared into aggressive action. Speeches and newspaper and magazine articles flooded both countries, though in the United States, opposition was the more vigorous. The main arguments were:

1. Need for a better waterway is not proved. Railroads can move all freight; if more are needed, build more.

2. If any waterway is constructed, it should be all American; Canada is friendly now, but why risk co-operative effort?

3. Benefits are greatly exaggerated. Grain exports are declining; soon all agricultural products will be needed by ourselves. In any case the proposed canal would be closed in winter and shippers would not be bothered with a short-season route.

4. The cost would be enormous—and would be assessed on all taxpayers in both countries, while the benefits would come to relatively few.

Other arguments were offered but were less important.

Such opposition strengthened the action *for* the improvements. The speeches and articles favorable to a deep waterway had four main points, too:

1. A demand *does* exist for a deep waterway. At least seventeen states will be directly affected; their population is about one third of the United States. Farmers, industrialists, and all recent presidents favor the work.

2. The national economy requires more transport. Railroad rates are high; railroad transport is inadequate, especially at crop-moving time.

3. Water transport is cheap and excellent for bulk products—ore, grain, coal, oil. The question is not between two sorts of transport; both rail and water are needed. The St. Lawrence Waterway is already in use; it needs only improving. The expense, while considerable, is small compared with benefits.

4. An improved waterway would bring ocean-going ships into the Middle West. The whole nation will benefit.

Other advantages were often mentioned: approval of competent engineers, sharing of construction and costs by the two

countries, the faith that new trade would develop. But the four
main points were always emphasized.

As the controversy went on, traffic at the Soo was heavy;
official figures showed that, in spite of ice which closed these locks
four or more months each year, the total tonnage at the Soo was
more than the *sum* of tonnage through the Panama, Suez, Kiel, and
Manchester canals in twelve months. The heart of North America
did not have a passage to Cathay, but it had a wealth of riches
going down and a great market for goods coming up.

Canada felt so sure that plans would go through that she began
building a new Welland Ship Canal (the fourth) with dimensions to
fit specifications of a proposed seaway—twenty-five foot depth.
The Canadians had wanted a twenty-seven foot depth, but the
United States objected, so Canada accepted the general plan.

The New Welland Ship Canal cost $130 million and was com-

Ships locking through twin locks of the Welland Ship Canal.

pleted in 1932; it has eight locks—three of a new twin model, remarkable then, and now. The locks are 80 feet wide, 859 feet long,
and 30 feet deep over the sills. This masterpiece gave access between the four upper lakes and Ontario, but was no help on east
—it even served to emphasize the bottleneck made by 22 locks on
the St. Lawrence that, with their connecting canals, were only 14
feet deep.

Somehow the near-magic of the powerful locks of the new
Welland revived faith in the idea of a seaway. And other events
were happening—power was entering the picture. While the Welland was building, the Beauharnois power plant, with canal and
locks, was begun down the St. Lawrence River; it took power from
the rapids in the Soulanges section. In 1936, the Hydro-Electric
Power Commission of Ontario requested additional diversion of
water at Niagara equal to that taken in the Ogoki watershed into
Lake Superior. The whole matter of waterway and power seemed
ready for action.

In such an atmosphere, engineers reported favorably, heads of
state were in agreement, and a Seaway Treaty between the United
States and Canada was signed in 1932. Senate approval by a two-
thirds vote seemed certain. However, various minority lobbies were
successful in delaying the vote, and when it was taken in 1934, it
was 46 to 42—far short of the two-thirds vote required for treaty
approval. Canada, though deeply disappointed, was not in a position just then to carry out the project alone. During the depression
years the idea was considered dead.

President Franklin D. Roosevelt, like most twentieth century
presidents regardless of party, was vigorously in favor of the seaway.
He revived the project in March of 1941 by entering into an agreement with Canada to construct power and navigation facilities on
the St. Lawrence. This agreement differed from a treaty in that it
needed only a majority vote of both houses for confirmation—he

was certain he could get that. The legality of this substitute agreement is still debated; but before it could be tested in the courts, Pearl Harbor and World War II intervened, and the project was again dropped. The president did make one effort toward action by executive order but was not able to get funds appropriated. After the war, Congress refused to approve the agreement, and again the project seemed dead and eternally embalmed in committees.

Then in the late 1940's several important events caught public attention. Rumor said that Mesabi ore was running short; sixty years earlier that would have seemed incredible, but two world wars and the expansion of the industrial age had used up iron in unbelievable quantities. And who would have guessed, in 1890, that there would *be* two world wars? Man was supposed to have reached a mature age of peaceful negotiation. Who foresaw automobiles—millions of automobiles? Who guessed the numbers of refrigerators, deep freezes, bridges, huge machines, and other needs for steel? "Unlimited" ore was running low. Before this came to public notice, farsighted men were working to forestall the famine. They discovered taconite, a low-grade iron ore, near Lake Superior; they built Silver Bay and other cities where new plants converted taconite into usable form. But a dozen cities along the lower lakes—Milwaukee, Chicago, Gary, Cleveland, Erie, among them—needed iron faster than taconite and the depleted Mesabi could supply it.

Steel men brought iron from South America, shipping to eastern ports and then by rail. But this made a long haul, vulnerable in case of war. A closer source of iron was needed.

In 1948 came exciting news that iron ore of the very best quality was discovered on the Labrador-Quebec border. A 400-mile haul by railroad would bring it to the St. Lawrence port city of Seven Islands—a relatively safe and cheap haul. The ore could go up the St. Lawrence past Quebec and Montreal; but what about those 22 short locks and the shallow, narrow canals? The long, low ore boats that came down from Lake Superior could not operate through those waterways.

Coincident with this revival of need for better navigation was the newly recognized need by both New York state and the province of Ontario for power from the international area of the great river.

Canada shrewdly saw that the time was ripe; there must be no further delay. She said politely but firmly that she would build an all-Canadian seaway of her own. She certainly could do it; her position was much stronger than in 1933, and the Welland Canal, a proved success, was already built. In 1951 the Canadian parliament passed the St. Lawrence Seaway Act, setting up the St. Lawrence Seaway Authority as agent to undertake the construction of a seaway entirely within Canadian borders. The Honourable Lionel Chevrier was appointed its president.

New York State, left out by this new plan, made a hasty attempt to meet power needs alone. But men of vision in the United States saw that hope for both power and navigation lay in joint effort.

Then the idea of tolls was tossed into the controversy. Neither nation had charged tolls—at the Soo or the Welland—the idea being that free navigation was for the benefit of all the people. But tolls, charged to repay the governments for construction and maintenance costs, would remove the objection that all taxpayers shared the cost while only a part received benefits. The toll idea was accepted quickly, indication of the discouragement felt since 1950 when President Truman urged a seaway act and congress adjourned without action. No definite amount was set for tolls; inflation had begun, and no one at that time dared estimate costs. But the plan was to charge as little as possible (to encourage use of the seaway), and yet enough to repay cost, interest, and maintenance in fifty years.

Seaway problems were still being debated when in 1952 the

state of New York and the province of Ontario made application to the International Joint Commission to construct a power dam in connection with the seaway. The application was approved, but a two-year legal battle was fought in the courts of New York before June 10, 1954, when permission was granted.

That same spring of 1954, congress passed the Wiley-Dondero Act setting up a new agency, The St. Lawrence Seaway Development Corporation, to work with Canada's agency and build the seaway. Lewis G. Castle of Duluth was appointed administrator.

On the 13th of May, 1954, a group of men assembled in President Eisenhower's office to witness the signing of this important act. Among those present were Canadian Ambassador A.P.T. Heeney, Senator Alexander Wiley of Wisconsin, and Congressman George A. Dondero of Michigan, co-authors of the act. As they entered the office, Senator Wiley remarked, "Across the river we have held hands; now we cannot part. We are one in a great adventure—to build for the future of America."

President Eisenhower picked up a pen to sign, then paused and said: "I think it is particularly fortunate that we have with us the Ambassador from Canada, because this bill is to set in motion the great project which will operate for the benefit of both our countries. . . . Now work can begin on the project itself . . . so that its benefits can come to all our people on both sides of the great river."

Jacques Cartier had discovered and named the gulf and the river on St. Lawrence' Day in 1535. On that same day in August, 1954, impressive ceremonies were held on both sides of the river in the international section. Distinguished guests from one country were invited to ceremonies of the other. Flags of both nations fluttered companionably near. In this friendly way Canada and the United States signified their intention to work together on the largest joint construction project ever attempted. Plans were long since ready. Now work could begin.

CHAPTER II

The Power Project

THE St. Lawrence Seaway begins at the Lake Erie entrance to the Welland Ship Canal, continues through that canal, crosses Lake Ontario, proceeds in the St. Lawrence River through several small lakes, which are really a part of the river, to a point just below the Jacques Cartier Bridge, the most easterly of the four bridges at Montreal, where it ends. The remaining distance of more than a thousand miles to the sea is already deep enough for ocean shipping.

Approaching from the west, the first section, the Welland Ship Canal, has eight locks of seaway size. There remained only to deepen the canal from 25 feet to the present requirement of 27 feet. This work was done and paid for by Canada.

Crossing Lake Ontario, a very deep basin, the seaway enters the St. Lawrence River; the drop from this point to the ocean is 225 feet, much of it in three areas of rapids—the Long Sault, the Soulanges, and the Lachine. Through the Thousand Islands section, the westerly part of the river, the fall is slight and the only work required was the deepening of the channel from 25 feet to 27. Most of this work has been done and paid for by the United States.

Further east, the water level falls a little more than 90 feet at the Long Sault Rapids, where the swift currents and countless rocks made hard going even for the skillful Indians. Here, at Iroquois Point, the power project, an important part in the entire plan, begins to share the river with the seaway.

Three huge structures are required for power: a control dam at Iroquois Point on the Canadian side, below Prescott; a powerhouse connecting Barnhart Island and the north shore of the river above Cornwall, Ontario; and a giant spillway a little south and west of the powerhouse which controls the depth of the power pool and the flow to the river on below.

The idea of using the fall of water to make power is not new; its discovery lies hidden in ancient times when man learned that buckets fastened on a water wheel turned by a river's current could irrigate his field.

Later men discovered that a grinding stone could be turned by the power of falling water; Hamilton Merritt's mills were operated by this method well into the nineteenth century. But a fall of water *at one place* was essential to the task. The 90-foot fall of the Long Sault was useless for power unless a deep pool was created and the fall made to come at one point—the powerhouse, where in the twentieth century the force of the fall is used to turn turbines to make electricity.

To make a power pool where once the Long Sault Rapids flowed would flood 18,000 acres on the American side, and displace more

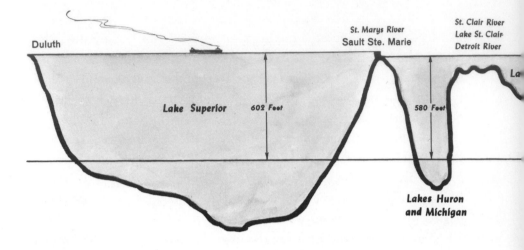

than 200 farms and 600 small homes. On the Canadian side the flooding would be even more disrupting, for canals had brought St. Lawrence commerce along the north shore; three towns, four villages, more than 200 farms, 40 miles of railroad and some 35 miles of highway must be moved to make the projected pool that was planned to be more than 30 miles long and one to four miles wide. Would people tolerate such dislocation of their lives?

The Hydro-Electric Power Commission of Ontario, Ontario Hydro for short, began their task early. As soon as plans for the seaway were assured in 1951 and the power project seemed likely, representatives, carrying maps, visited every family, every business, school, and church that would be affected. The project was explained, and then a question was asked.

"Will you help? Will you move back from the river three or four miles? We will build you a new house, about the size of this one, in a new town; we will install plumbing and electricity. Or, if you want to stay in this house, we will move it, set it on a new concrete foundation, and put in plumbing and electricity. The cost

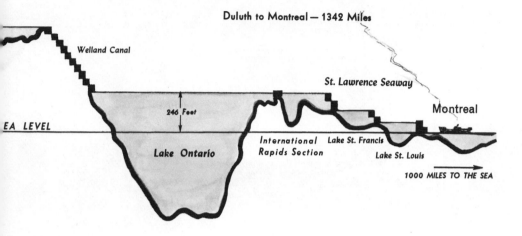

Duluth to Montreal — 1342 Miles

Welland Canal

St. Lawrence Seaway

Montreal

SEA LEVEL

246 Feet

Lake Ontario

International Rapids Section

Lake St. Francis

Lake St. Louis

1000 MILES TO THE SEA

of either plan you choose will be paid jointly by Ontario Hydro and the Power Authority of the State of New York, who are constructing the new power project."

This was not an easy question to answer; people had lived for years by the river; their living was there, their neighbors.

"The railroad and the highway will be moved back," the questioner went on, encouragingly, "a modern town and shopping center will be laid out."

The young people, it is said, welcomed the excitement of change; older people were reluctant, but to their credit they did not block the move. The idea was not unexpected. Plans had been talked of for a long time. But that very length of time had made the idea unreal; what is "some day" need not be decided; now the questioner was at the door.

Ingleside, Morrisburg, Iroquois, and four villages agreed to move. In a way it was a relief to have uncertainty end and to make definite decisions.

At Old Iroquois (the name given the town to be flooded) one

(Above) A house being moved from the old town of Iroquois to the site of the new community, one and one half miles north. This is one of 525 houses moved by Ontario Hydro. (Right) The same house has been placed on its new foundation. Soon after, electric, telephone, and water services were connected, and the family resumed normal living.

hundred and two families wanted to have their houses moved; the others chose new dwellings. Sites were selected in the newly laid-out area, back, on higher land. Plans were made and approved. Work began. Machines and equipment for moving one hundred and two houses arrived along with the builders of new buildings. Buildings not moved, trees, posts, and other things, would be razed, including a long business block facing the once busy canal.

Ontario Hydro's representatives went through the whole area—the 30 miles of the north shore of the future power pool—and marked each building, large or small, with a number. A farm corn crib by the Long Sault, for instance, might be marked 3175; each one of the four figures gave workmen directions as to whether that building was to be moved or razed, and when. Every structure had its turn in a colossal effort at fairness. Only two buildings were left standing, and these were back on the edge of Old Iroquois; one was the century-old Carver house, a treasured landmark in the area. The waters of the new lake come near but do not touch the doorstone.

Actual moving time was exciting. The movers prided themselves upon their skill and on their care for a family's possessions. A crew arrived at one house, early, to find the family eating breakfast.

"Don't get up!" the head mover called casually. "Go on and eat. We're just moving the house."

Some people tacked signs on their houses:

WE HAVE TO GO, BUT WATCH US GROW!

And for the journey, families walked alongside the house.

"So you're going!" neighbors called. "Hope our turn comes tomorrow."

Other families set lamps, clocks, and vases on the floor, then, breakfast finished, they stacked the dishes till the plumbing was in and watched the journey from a window. Once settled on a new cement foundation, it took a little time to get a garden planted and feel at home in the new neighborhood.

On a sunny afternoon in August of 1957, automobiles with licenses from several states and provinces were chancing partly barricaded Old Road Number 2 by the canal when they came upon Morrisburg in the act of being moved. Here a machine was cutting through brick foundation walls, inserting jacks to raise the house; next door the jacks had done their work and the house was on rollers, ready to go. Down the street a huge machine roared and pulled, trying to get a reluctant house started. The long dry spell, good for work on the great structures in the river bed, had turned the road to deep dust with no purchase for the machine's tires. They slid and slithered; the house did not move. Tourists, delighted to arrive in the midst of action, parked their cars helter-skelter and ran to the scene, cameras ready. Again the machine roared; again the house did not move.

"Where's it going, when it goes?" a man with an Arizona license asked.

"Up the road to New Town—about three miles." Any new site was New Town—Iroquois, Morrisburg, Ingleside.

"Do the people who own that house really want to move?" a traveler from Ohio wondered. That question troubled many people who drove along there that summer.

"Well, now," the workman turned and gave thoughtful attention to the inquiry, "they get their choice—some choice, anyway. They get a new house, about the same size but new style, with plumbing and electricity and everything nice. Or they get their old house moved—like this one—and fixed up."

"How wonderful," someone in the group exclaimed fervently, and looked with acute disfavor at the stubborn house that did not move. "Of course they take the new."

"It is not 'of course,'" the workman said politely enough, but with a hint of irritation. "Up at Old Iroquois—have you been there? —more than a hundred folks liked their own houses better than new ones. Those old houses, moved and fixed up, do something for a town. It isn't good to have everything new; seems too sudden."

"People gain a lot by moving," someone remarked.

The workman studied that a minute; then he asked, "Would you think you gained if you'd lived all your life by the canal and had to leave it? If you had watched ships day after day and had to move so bigger ships and electricity could come? Would you like to live miles back where you couldn't see a thing that was going on? Plumbing—we didn't miss it. What's a new foundation if you leave the ships? Makes a man wonder. They tell us it's for the good of all. I didn't object. That next house there is mine. We're going tomorrow."

The machine roared. Wheels caught this time. Slowly, steadily, the house moved toward the road, and men leaped to adjust rollers.

A ship in the Cornwall Canal passing the International Rapids. After this picture was taken, this section was pumped dry during the construction of the Long Sault Dam.

"You'll all have to move your cars," the foreman said politely. "We're coming down that way."

While the moving of towns was going on, contractors and hundreds of workmen arrived to start building the dam, the spillway, and the powerhouse. Upriver from where Iroquois Dam was to be, dikes and a cofferdam turned the mighty river into a southern channel. Just below the powerhouse site, the largest cofferdam in the world was built—a mile of huge metal tubes filled to the brim with excavated soil and gravel. Over by the spillway a third cofferdam guided the river's flow south. Some idea of the quantity of water diverted can be realized when one remembers that 236,000 cubic feet of water per second flow down from Lake Ontario.

But that mass of water no longer dashed over and around giant boulders of the Long Sault; the rapids no longer sang, and no more rainbows glinted in the mist above the foam. Down by the powerhouse, cofferdam pumps cleared out the last remnant of water so that building of the three structures could begin. In 1957, the Long Sault river bed, more than 30 miles long, was dry dust, a sandy monotone that did not even make a good photograph—a strange sight to anyone who had "shot the rapids." The river bed looked like a gash—an affront to nature.

Work on Iroquois Dam started early; the first concrete was poured in November of 1955. The purpose of this dam is to regulate the flow of water from Lake Ontario. Located at Point Iroquois, Canada, across from Point Rockaway, in the United States, it is a buttressed gravity-type dam with 32 openings between piers; the vertical-lift gates are operated by 35-ton traveling gantry cranes.

The mate of Iroquois Dam is the Long Sault Spillway Dam, built at the foot of Long Sault Island about three miles southwest of the powerhouse. Its function is to control the amount of water in the power pool—the man-made lake—and to release the proper amount for the river below.

All the new construction along the St. Lawrence has a certain beauty, but this long, curving spillway dam is a poem in concrete. It has 30 gates, each 50 feet wide; 18 have fixed hoists, and 12 are operated by a traveling crane which moves along as needed on the top of the dam. The first concrete on this structure was poured in October of 1955. Because of very complicated problems in the diversion of the river, the spillway was built in sections and was finished in ample time for the filling of the power pool.

The making of the power pool, the Lake St. Lawrence, was a dramatic scene in mid-1958, arranged to celebrate Dominion Day in Canada, July first, and Independence Day in the United States, July fourth. Thirty tons of dynamite were buried deep in the last cofferdam upstream from Barnhart Island Power House. Crowds

The graceful arc of the Long Sault Dam, stretching from the New York state mainland to a point near the head of Barnhart Island.

Gaping holes were blasted in this 600-foot cofferdam on July 1, 1958. Water ripped away the rest of the dam, as it rushed on its way to form the power pool, Lake St. Lawrence.

watched from both shores on the morning of July first when an electrical current touched off the dynamite and blew up the final barrier.

For a few instants the river seemed to hesitate. Then, as the air cleared, the freed water rushed over the debris into the old river bed. Dust vanished. Age-old stones were covered. Water deepened back of the powerhouse and began to spread, beginning the lake that covered old banks, former streets and towns and farms.

Day and night the water flowed—spreading wide, deepening.

On July second, the United States held dedication ceremonies at the two new locks, now filling. On the fourth, the U.S. Coast Guard Cutter *Maple* had the honor of passing through the locks and the canal, eastbound. Several other government vessels followed. The first commercial ship through the locks was the Canadian S.S. *Humberdoc*, westbound. In the first week 263 ships from ten nations used the locks.

Celebrating the opening of this part of the seaway, Cornwall welcomed thousands of visitors as did Massena in her three-day Vacationland Festival July 4th week end. Visitors joined residents in marveling at the new convincing evidence of the power of men and machines in remaking the face of the earth and adapting its waters to the service of mankind.

The powerhouse just west of Cornwall, Ontario, connects Barnhart Island with the north shore of the river and straddles exactly the international line between Canada and the United States. It is actually one building, 3,300 feet long; all during the years of construction it was called Barnhart Powerhouse. But because of that

The Robert Moses Power Dam and the Robert H. Saunders—St. Lawrence Generating Station.

imaginary line, it is often spoken of as two powerhouses and in the
end bears two names. The Canadian section is the Robert H.
Saunders—St. Lawrence Generating Station, honoring the late

The Moses—Saunders powerhouse under construction. In the foreground is
shown the concrete for the turbines; in the background, the pit liners for several of the units can be seen. In the far background, the first generator is being
assembled.

Mr. Saunders, who worked for years on the power project. The United States half of the building is called Robert Moses Power Dam, honoring the chairman of the Power Authority of New York. The companion structure, the spillway dam, is officially named Long Sault Dam.

One of the intake portals of the powerhouse. The size of the portal can be judged by comparing it to the men. Each of the 32 turbines will receive water from three such openings.

The building has 32 generators and produces 2,200,000 horsepower of electricity (1,880,000 k.h.), which, like all costs, are equally divided between the two co-operating agencies, Ontario Hydro and the Power Authority of New York. The building is a thrilling sight. Long, graceful, mighty, it rears up from the end of the power pool. Observation and reception rooms are on the roof at each end. On the roof, too, great traveling cranes move on rails. During construction they lifted vast amounts of heavy material; now they raise or lower gates, controlling the operations of the turbines. The flags of the two nations fly only a few feet apart, at the middle of the building. At the moment of its opening it was the second largest powerhouse in the world—Grand Coulee is slightly larger—and it is the only powerhouse that is built, maintained, and shared by governments of two nations.

From this powerhouse huge steel towers, looking like spider webs against a summer sky, carry strong wires bearing needed electricity far and wide to homes, to towns, to industries—a boon to the people, a promise of jobs and better living.

CHAPTER 12

A Laker on the Seaway

THE three buildings of the power project are huge and dramatic. But the seaway is there, too, on the very same stretch of river; the seaway was in men's minds first, and its benefits can add to the prosperity of seventeen or more states, several provinces, and many nations. Ships, big ships, belong with a big river. Anyone who has watched the ocean-going ships at Montreal or Quebec feels excited at the thought of some of these ships coming up into the lakes and of the long lakers going down. But the manner of this coming and going was not simple to provide.

After the Canadian bill for a seaway passed in 1951, Canadian engineers on the St. Lawrence Seaway Authority began work. On the passing of the United States bill in the spring of 1954, members of the St. Lawrence Seaway Development Corporation, began work. A first step was to request the United States Army Corps of Engineers to design needed structures, to write specifications, and to act as the contracting agency for the corporation. This was done September 2nd, less than a month after the formal starting ceremonies. The engineers began these important duties, and the corporation had the responsibility of examining, approving, and of keeping the public informed as to progress and spending. Actual construction was done by private contractors, who submitted bids for all phases of the work.

The army engineers could begin work immediately because they had long been studying navigation problems in seaway con-

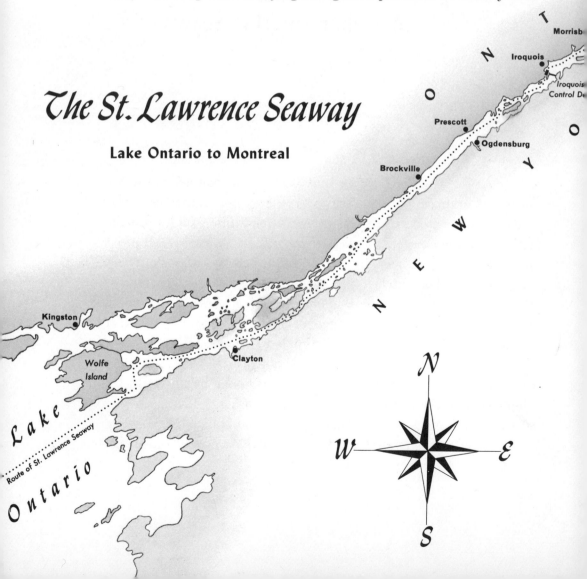

The St. Lawrence Seaway

Lake Ontario to Montreal

KEY

1 Cornwall Canal
2 Moses-Saunders Powerhouse
3 Barnhart Island
4 Long Sault Dam
5 Eisenhower Lock
6 Wiley-Dondero Canal
7 Snell Lock
8 International High Level Bridge
9 Cornwall Island
10 Beauharnois Lock
11 C.P.R. Bridge
12 Honoré-Mercier Bridge
13 Victoria Bridge
14 St. Lambert Lock

struction. On that September day they were ready. Studies included tests on hydraulic models at the Army's Experiment Station at Vicksburg, Mississippi, where currents in the St. Lawrence, rates of flow, direction of placing locks, and scores of other problems that might some day come up for decision were worked out. The army has another station in Minneapolis; Canada has the National Research Laboratory at Ottawa; and Ontario Hydro has a laboratory at Islington, Ontario. Engineers of both countries worked together, and to avoid duplication of effort, different problems were assigned to different laboratories and representatives of both nations were present when tests were run.

One of the problems the models solved was the location and the amount of land that would be flooded by the making of the power pool at the Long Sault. Experiments were so accurate that when flooding began in 1958, the new towns, railroads, and highways were exactly where they were expected to be in relation to the new lake. There had been no guessing.

The currents of water in the power pool are so planned that

in winter, when ice forms, it will not be too thick nor will it obstruct the even flow of water to the turbines in the powerhouse.

Ships must cross the power pool—where? At what angle? With what currents? So perfectly are currents and other details worked out that if, later, the United States wants to build a lock bypassing Iroquois Dam, or Canada wants a lock by the north shore, bypassing the powerhouse, the work can be done without waste of extra costs for alterations.

With the seaway complete and at its full depth, a great laker will leave the upper lakes with a bulk cargo of, say, grain from the prairies. She will pass through the Welland Ship Canal and locks, cross Lake Ontario, travel some eighty miles down the St. Lawrence to Iroquois Point, and there come to the first power structure, Iroquois Dam, and the first seaway structure, Iroquois Lock, which bypasses the dam. This lock, a single one, as the drop in water level

Two passenger ships, the *South American* and the *North American*, were the first cruise ships and the first ships to exceed 14-foot draft to lock through the seaway. They are entering the Eisenhower Lock.

is only six feet, cuts right through Iroquois Point just north of the dam and sets the laker down at the west end of the power pool. Iroquois Lock is the most westerly of seven new locks and is one of five built and paid for by Canada.

On through the power pool, more than thirty miles long, the grain boat proceeds east and slightly south as it angles toward the United States part of the river. A deep, well-defined channel avoids sharp turns and speeds navigation as the laker approaches the area of the powerhouse and the spillway but well to the south of these power structures. Soon the laker enters a canal and comes to a lock, a connecting canal, and a second lock; these locks each lift or lower 45 feet—a total of 90-foot drop brought to the powerhouse for creating electricity. The parts of the seaway the laker is now using—the canal and two locks—were built and paid for by the United States.

These locks are 860 feet long, 80 feet wide, and 30 feet deep. The usable length—the distance between the miter gates, which are opened and closed as the ships are raised and lowered in the lock chamber—is 768 feet. Canadian locks down the river are about these same dimensions.

At the beginning of the work on the seaway, traditional, local names were used for these structures; the western lock was Robinson Bay Lock because of its location by a bay of that name; the canal was the Long Sault Canal and the eastern lock was Grass River Lock because the Grass River enters the St. Lawrence nearby. But as work progressed, many people felt that these two locks and their canal, the only portion of the seaway that was entirely the work of the United States, offered the best chance to honor men who had done service in making the seaway possible. So, in 1956, Robinson Bay Lock was renamed the Dwight D. Eisenhower Lock. President Eisenhower was the last of many presidents who had worked for a seaway, and he was the one who signed the act that brought it into

The Eisenhower Lock Tunnel carries traffic to Barnhart Island. Ships in the seaway pass over the tunnel.

being. Two years later Grass River Lock was renamed the Bertrand H. Snell Lock, in honor of Congressman Snell of New York, who introduced the first bill; and the canal was named the Wiley-Dondero Canal, in honor of Senator Wiley and Congressman Dondero, who wrote the final bill and got it passed. The Eisenhower and Snell locks, three and one-half miles apart in the ten-mile-long canal, are identical except that a highway tunnel runs under the Eisenhower Lock conveying traffic to Barnhart Island.

South of the canal and locks is the little city of Massena, New York, a place that has gained much by all this rush of construction in its neighborhood. Massena gets electricity from the river by means of the Massena Intake, a narrow canal flowing southward, which is said to be the first use of power taken from the river. The aluminum industry which used power—along with Massena—has grown so large that it now buys from the Power Authority of the state of New York, but the old Intake, somewhat modified, continues to supply Massena with electricity for domestic and community uses.

Here in Massena, too, is the handsome new Operations Building, headquarters for the St. Lawrence Seaway Development Corporation. The agency moved from Washington, D.C., in 1958.

Across the river beyond the locks, the spillway, and the powerhouse, is the busy city of Cornwall, Ontario. The names of these two cities carry on the French and English traditions—Cornwall thoroughly English; Massena named for a French general, famous in the Napoleonic wars. In Cornwall a beautiful steel and glass, eight-story building is the headquarters for the Canadian agency, The St. Lawrence Seaway Authority.

But the laker is leaving the Snell Lock, let down 45 feet into the South Channel of the river, now deepened to the 27-foot clearance. As it gains speed it passes under the new International Bridge —a high-level suspension bridge with the 120-foot clearance required for ships on the seaway. This new bridge is one of the unique features of the seaway; it replaces the low-level bridge which connected New York State with Cornwall Island and was adequate when the 14-foot canal was along the north shore. When the old bridge was demolished, a bronze plaque, placed to honor the friendship of Canada and the United States, was removed and saved. Its inscription read:

> "This unfortified boundary line between the Dominion of Canada and the United States of America should quicken the remembrance of the more than century-old friendship between the two countries, a lesson of peace to all nations. Erected July 14, 1936. Kiwanis International."

This plaque is reinstalled on the new bridge.

More remarkable even than formal words is the spirit of cooperation in the actual building of the handsome new bridge; Canada built the substructure and the United States, the superstructure. Jointly the two nations own the Cornwall International Bridge Company and share in the operation as well as the ownership of the bridge.

A short way downriver from the bridge the international line leaves the river and cuts off east over hills and mountains to the Atlantic Ocean. The remaining long reaches of the seaway were constructed and paid for by Canada; the division of total costs is about one third for the United States and two thirds for Canada. From the end of South Channel, near Lake St. Francis, all bridges, tunnels, channels, locks, and canals are under the direction of The St. Lawrence Seaway Authority.

As the laker comes into beautiful Lake St. Francis, it enters a quiet stretch so welcome to early navigators, worn from fighting through the rapids. For thirty miles a ship proceeds on an almost straight line to the western end of the Beauharnois Power Canal, dredged now to the 27-foot depth. Toward the eastern end of this canal, two handsome locks bypass the Beauharnois powerhouse; the fall of water here by the Soulanges Rapids is about 82 feet, and each lock lifts or lowers half that distance. These locks are essentially like the Eisenhower and the Snell locks upriver. Under the downriver lock is a tunnel with a four-lane highway so that highway traffic and ship traffic do not interrupt each other.

Beyond the Beauharnois section ships go through the quiet waters of Lake St. Louis to the Lachine Rapids section—a part of the river that challenged the Indians, the French, and today's engineers. The Canadian engineers chose a new route that brings the seaway along the south side of the rapids instead of the north, nearer to the city of Montreal; but in this new approach, many difficulties had to be overcome. Four great bridges connect the north and south shores of the river: one, the Canadian Pacific Railway Bridge; close by it, the Honoré Mercier Highway Bridge; downriver, the Victoria Bridge, carrying highway and the Canadian National

Railway; and last, the Jacques Cartier Bridge, carrying heavy high-way traffic, not only within Canada but from the United States. These bridges were relatively low-level; the old canals were across to the north. All were sound, and alteration rather than costly rebuilding was begun.

A new section was built on the south end of each bridge; vertical lifts and new approaches are so designed that later, if necessary, high-level bridges can be built. Victoria Bridge is provided with two vertical lifts, with new approaches and an extensive system of traffic signals which guides highway traffic to the approach not being used at the moment for passage of ships. Also the Canadian National Railway expects to build a separate railway approach.

One of the most dramatic operations on the entire seaway was the remaking of the Jacques Cartier Bridge, which leads its continuous flow of traffic into the heart of Montreal. The bridge over the end of the seaway must be raised 80 feet; traffic must not be interrupted—how was this miracle accomplished?

Work began on new, higher approaches. In the summer of

Raising the Jacques Cartier Bridge, one of those which span the seaway channel at Montreal.

1957, hundreds of men and machines worked south of the bridge—
yet the seeming confusion was orderly construction; traffic was
seldom stopped, and then only three hours at a time—1 to 4 A.M.
at previousiy announced dates. Men worked on the 250-foot span
of the bridge, too, even as traffic flowed by. New through truss-
spans were set to replace deck-trusses, the new work put in place
above and below the roadway on the bridge. Supports were set on
rollers. On October 20, 1957, hydraulic jacks lifted the 1500 tons
of the old span away and set the 1600 tons of the new in place.
This gained 30 feet. The strength of the new span allowed re-
moval of the former undersupports and gained the additional 50-
foot clearance—the whole a marvel of technical skill.

Other problems as the seaway neared the city included ar-
rangements with the Indians at the Caughnawaga Indian Reservation—the site of the one time Iroquois village across from La Salle's
land and now touching the new approaches to the Canadian Pacific
and the Honoré Mercier bridges. By the treaty of 1763 this land,
now the reservation, was given to the Six Nation Confederacy as an
independent nation—completely surrounded by Canada. Caughnawaga issues its own passports; Chief Diome was alert in protecting
his people's rights. The use of a strip of land for the seaway canal
and the new bridge approaches was a matter of careful negotiation.
Compared with bridges and Caughnawaga, other problems, such as
protecting water and sewer outlets for Montreal and several villages,
seem simple and have been solved.

The seaway itself leaves the river above the Lachine Rapids
and enters a canal dug across the south shore of the area of the La
Prairie Basin. There Côte Ste. Catherine Lock lifts or lowers ships
30 feet to a different kind of canal, made by high dikes and parallel
to the south shore of the basin. These dikes, like others along the
seaway, are made of glacial till—hard as cement—gravel, and earth;
they look and are new, raw, and safe. Time will weather them and

The massive concrete walls of the St. Lambert Lock, the most easterly of the locks on the seaway route.

make them a fitting part of the beautiful view across from the seaway to Montreal, the city on the mountainside.

By Victoria Bridge, St. Lambert Lock lifts or lowers ships the final 22 feet, and the canal leads to the two large turn-arounds for ship-maneuvering south of the busy wharfs on the north shore and on down the river.

All this complicated work was completed well before the grain boat left its harbor in the upper country, its hold filled with newly harvested grain. With ease and not the slightest delay, the laker left the river, entered the canal, was set down by Côte Ste. Catherine Lock and a few minutes later by St. Lambert Lock. Bridges raised briefly as the laker moved by, passed under the Jacques Cartier Bridge and into the wide, deep St. Lawrence. The final thousand miles of her 2342-mile journey was nature's gift to navigation—an open, safe, sheltered way to the sea.

CHAPTER 13

Men and Machines

Hᴏᴡ many men worked on the seaway-power project?

It will be a wonder if the total is ever exactly known. Scores
of private contractors had forces varying from half a dozen men
to hundreds, working around the clock. Innumerable government
officials worked in many cities, as well as along the river; here and
there a lonely dredge worked steadily, the small crew digging away
to make that 27-foot requirement. The official estimate of the
workers is 22,000—but of course that figure tells only part of
the story. Add to that 22,000 all the men and women in factories
who made the hundreds of machines used on the job; add to these
all the men who brought the machines to the job—by rail, truck,
ship, and barge; add to these the foreign workers who made special

parts; turbines in Germany, steel parts in Italy; add the crews of transport ships—the number of workers is legion, certainly many times the 22,000 who actually worked on the river.

Before all these thousands of workers arrived, people along the river were concerned about so many strangers coming. Would they be good neighbors in their off-duty hours? Fears proved groundless: workers brought wives and children; they joined churches and local organizations. Their good pay brought prosperity to the river area. Thousands of workers found homes in towns and villages on both sides of the river and in 78 trailer camps. At first it was thought that because of the press of time—the power project was to be finished in 1958 and the seaway in 1959—work must be carried on seven

Work on the Long Sault Dam and other parts of the power project continued day and night, six days a week, in order to maintain the construction schedule.

days a week. But some experimenting and careful records showed that more work was actually accomplished when *all* workers rested on the seventh day, so a six-day week held for everyone. But through the season of good weather each year, work continued around the clock. At the hours of shift, 8 A.M., 4 P.M., and midnight, good automobiles jammed the highways as men went to and from the job.

While this pleasant picture is true of the whole, some areas faced harder conditions. On the Canadian shore, uprooted towns and villages had serious problems which the nearby city of Cornwall, accustomed to ships, tourists, and trade, solved quickly. Across the river in the international area, New York towns and villages never had had a canal close by, nor any shipping. The seaway was long anticipated; then suddenly workers appeared in vast numbers—Massena's population of 14,000 doubled in a few months. How could a town prepare for such numbers in advance? Massena didn't. When the workers, contractors, and engineers came so quickly, problems of housing, parking, schools, merchandising, health, roads, and countless other matters were overwhelming. But though the little city staggered, it rose and met its challenge effectively.

It is indeed fortunate that several nationally known companies that intend to build new plants in the surrounding area wisely chose to delay such construction until the seaway and power project were about complete. Anticipation of new work tended to hold the population steady and to refute the argument, "Oh, they'll not be staying!" that would have indefinitely postponed solution of civic problems.

But men on the job and their families were not the only people who crowded into the international section. History repeats itself in the keen interest about work in progress. When the first Welland Canal was being built, neighbors walked to see what was going on. At the Soo, during the building of that first canal, hundreds came

up the St. Marys River on vacation to see the sights. In the later
1950's, automobiles had made travel commonplace; thousands came
to watch the technical miracles taking shape along the St. Lawrence
River. And they all asked questions—millions of questions.

To meet the insistent desire of the public to see and to be informed, Ontario Hydro set up an Information Center by the highway, west of Cornwall; they trained guides—high-school teachers,
graduate students, and others carefully selected for skill in meeting this touring public. A few guides spoke several languages;
many were bilingual. French was needed not only for visitors
from the province of Quebec but for some who came from France,
where there is keen interest in the seaway.

In the Center, walls were covered with blow-ups of photographs of the work; every hour a short movie about the project
was followed by a bus trip to the powerhouse out on the dry and
dusty river—all free to the public.

During a summer in the midst of construction, almost a million
tourists visited this Center; they gained accurate information and
some understanding of the sights they saw. Parked cars carried
licenses from every state and province and from several foreign
countries.

On one of its trips, the bus sped along the route on Highway 2
toward the powerhouse. Visitors saw huge metal gates painted
brilliant orange-red for weather protection and stacked like cord-
wood in a vacant lot. Before the next summer those gates were set
in the powerhouse by huge gantry cranes traveling on the powerhouse roof. Beyond the pile of gates the bus made a quick turn and
dropped down into a tunnel under the "old canal." There were two
tunnels—one for automobiles and buses, one for trucks with materials; a major problem was that of keeping the old canal open
for navigation while new work was going on. That problem continued until the summer of 1958 when the old canals were flooded

out and ships used the new locks and the new power pool.

But the bus was moving on—out of the tunnel it labored up to the top of the cofferdam, that mile-long row of metal cylinders filled with spoil from excavations. Perhaps nothing in all the work on the river shows more dramatically the advance in technology in a century than does a mental comparison between this cofferdam, now taken away, its work completed, and Charles Harvey's hastily improvised cofferdam of sailcloth and gravel.

On the high level by the powerhouse, people spilled out of the bus while the guide explained the busy scene. Workmen swarmed everywhere.

"The men wear helmets of different colors," someone noticed.

"A man's job is shown by the color of his helmet," the guide

The mile-long cofferdam that held back the waters of the St. Lawrence River during construction of the Moses–Saunders powerhouse. This view was taken looking north at the structure from the United States end.

Visitors to the Ontario Hydro half of the powerhouse are standing on one of the cofferdam cylinders. Ontario Hydro provided free transportation and guides for the thousands of visitors who came to see the work in progress.

said. "Carpenters wear yellow—hundreds of carpenters are needed to build forms for concrete and to build various temporary structures. Concrete workers wear green helmets; steel workers, blue; electrical workers, a different shade of bright blue; office workers, white; mechanical workers, silver; special mechanics, multicolored. The organization suggests an army, a field office with engineers, technicians, staff workers, and the labor crew."

Cameras were clicking as the guide answered dozens of questions.

"Where's the boss?" a visitor asked, looking around.

"Boss?" the guide was puzzled. "You mean the contractor? There are many contractors. You see . . . "

"No, I don't see. I'm from Michigan. Now, when we built the first locks and canals, Charles Harvey walked up and down that mile of land and kept track of everything. Even when the last lock was built—the MacArthur—the boss was right there. You could see him looking after everything."

"I've read about your locks," the guide said, as the Michigan man paused. "But you see, sir, this job is different. The part of it for the making of electricity is about thirty-five miles long, and then there is the seaway, too, widening it out. The seaway on this river is 114 miles long. The 'bosses' are two nations, a province and a state; each of those have 'agencies'—there is the St. Lawrence Seaway Development Corporation and . . . "

"Oh, those long names! I mean one boss."

The guide smiled. "No one man could attend to all of this, sir. It's done by teamwork; by dividing up the job so that, working together, everything comes out right and on time. Teamwork; that's the twentieth century way to do a big job."

"I think I begin to see," a man nearby remarked. "I've been trying to take a picture, and I can't get it all in—not even this one powerhouse, not as I'd like to have it. I'd have to be up in an airplane to get a view, a really good view."

"That's right, sir," the guide agreed. "No man can walk up and down and boss *this* job on the spot. He has to stand off a bit—in Washington or Ottawa; he has to know the blueprints and study reports to know how we're getting on." The young man glanced at his watch. "If you're ready now, we'll be returning to the Center."

Most of the visitors were silent as the bus went back, through the tunnel, along the highway by the stacked gates; the dignity and scope of the undertaking was overwhelming. Arrived at the Center, they studied the huge outdoor map with new understanding and then moved on to other points along the work, determined to see and to learn about the whole project, and to come back when the seaway was open and see exactly how those huge structures functioned.

Across the river at Massena a small group of visitors drove out on Route 37 to a contractor's office and from there, with a guide, visited the powerhouse from the United States side of the river. A long temporary bridge led to Barnhart Island and the United States end of the structure and the cofferdam. On this second visit to the powerhouse, the building had begun to seem more real—less like a dream. Standing there, watching the two flags, there comes a sense of pride in this evidence of friendship and co-operation; *that* is no dream! On this spot in the great river, friendship is as real as the concrete poured into forms to make a dam.

The spillway was half finished in 1957, and hundreds of tons of crystal clear water poured through the beautiful crescent-shaped dam.

A few miles away at the Eisenhower Lock, the visitors saw trucks and tractors moving about on the sandy level, leaving behind them strange marks reminiscent of the tracks of prehistoric animals along the sandy beaches of the Great Lakes. From one of the overlooks, the two locks, the spillway, and the powerhouse could be seen—the structures that harness the mighty river and make it serve the people.

Seen together the realization comes that man, with his own strength, could never have done the job this scene reveals. It was possible only because men have learned to make machines to do what had been impossible. Machines of many sorts moved about— some fast, some slow-moving and powerful. A few were easy to identify: draglines, trucks, dredges, diesel shovels.

"Look down, right here," the guide said, and named machines:
> "Bulldozers, churn drills, hydraulic jacks,
> Big-bladed scrapers, rock wagons,
> Gantry cranes, trucks, 10-ton buckets,
> Pile drivers ... "

The words flowed on like lines in a modern poem, naming machines without which such structures as those along the seaway could never have been built.

Some of the machines that have worked on the seaway have come to have interesting names and personalities. The dredge *Gaillard* worked at deepening South Channel and then moved on to a short job on the Grass River approach. Probably the *Gentleman from Kentucky*, a dragline, is the most widely known—his name and fame have been written up in newspapers and magazines. The *Gentleman* was at his home, a mining section of Kentucky, when he was needed on the St. Lawrence River. Loaded onto two lashed-together steel barges, he rode to work by way of the Ohio and Mississippi rivers, the Illinois Waterway, the Great Lakes, the Welland Canal, and the upper St. Lawrence River—2,000 miles. The weight of the bucket, empty, is 14 tons, and on the last stages of his journey to work, all the skill of Captain George A. Wood of Ogdensburg was needed to finish off the trip safely. The *Gentleman* had the honor of moving the first earth in the Long Sault section of the seaway.

Crowds gathered to watch this first bit of earth lifted—people were not yet used to the powerful machines that would be commonplace by another year. The driver sat like a king, high in his cab, master of the digging. At a signal the huge bucket rose high, swung around, dropped down and bit into the earth, taking a 20-ton bite, and then swung high, and dumped the spoil into waiting trucks.

The honor of finishing the job on the South Channel went to the United States army engineers' favorite, the dredge *Paraiso*. This dredge was laid up in Panama when the engineers decided her skill was needed to finish in time for the opening of the United States locks in 1958. So *Paraiso* was loaded on an especially made dry dock for her journey across the Gulf of Mexico. Up the Missis-

(Above) One of the massive dredges at work in the Lake St. Louis section of the seaway. (Below) The *Gentleman from Kentucky*, a 650-ton dragline, moved the first earth in the Long Sault section.

A giant crawler tractor moving earth and rocks before construction of the Long Sault Dam.

sippi and the Illinois Waterway and on the Great Lakes, she went under her own power. To make ready for the Illinois part of the journey, portions of the superstructure were taken down, for the clearance under fixed bridges is only 28 feet. Then word was sent ahead, and as *Paraiso* went up the waterway, every lift bridge on the course was raised for her passing. After refitting, *Paraiso* did a little test-digging in the Detroit River to make sure her long crane and the scoop-bucket that lifts 15 cubic yards from the depths at one dip and her various other facilities were in order; then she went to work on the St. Lawrence River channel near the International Bridge.

In 1958 the new maintenance vessels built for work on the seaway were given the names dropped when the Snell and Eisenhower Locks were renamed. The tug *Robinson Bay*, made at Sturgeon Bay, Wisconsin, is especially designed for its various jobs; it has fire-fighting equipment, a derrick for taking snags out of the river, and an icebreaker—a very useful tug. The other vessel, *Grass River*, is a 150-foot-long gate-lifter derrick, built in Buffalo; it can lift 300 tons on its main hoist and 100 tons on a smaller hoist. It will stand by, ready to move lock gates in any emergency.

During construction, a thrilling sight was the glow of brilliant lights through the night. From the bank of the old canal, west of Cornwall, lights on the powerhouse four miles west could be seen gleaming brightly. By day, this view was a blur of sand-colored dust, hardly noticed. But by night! Great arc lights shone so clearly that each could be counted, and over the huge building flood lights appeared to draw the scene close—surely it was not four miles away?

Off to the left, some three miles further on, the lights on the spillway brightened the sky. At such a distance, individual lights are lost, but the myriads of arc lights seemed to flame up to the sky. Still further to the left, a faint glow told that men were working on the Eisenhower Lock, where shifts around the clock were needed to keep to schedule.

After construction was finished, these particular lights could no longer be seen. But because of the seaway, lights continue to flame into the sky above steel mills at Cleveland, Gary, Sault Sainte Marie, and many other places around the lakes. By way of the seaway iron ore can reach the mills from any place in the world, assuring jobs for thousands of workers.

CHAPTER 14

Channels and Harbors

As time moved along toward the opening of the seaway in 1959, people around the lakes talked about the sights they soon would be seeing—the big ships with foreign flags coming to lake ports. Lewis G. Castle, administrator of the St. Lawrence Development Corporation, felt impelled to say a word of warning:

"The seaway will be no magic wand bringing abundant prosperity on completion. Careful, realistic, frugal planning will be essential for every lake port." He knew that three or more years of work must be done before the expectation of new shipping and commercial advantages would be fully realized.

Because, in 1959, not a single Great Lakes channel, not one harbor, could match the 27-foot depth then available all the length of the seaway. A large ocean vessel, or a heavily loaded boat with ore from Labrador could come up the seaway to its end at the Welland Canal and Lake Erie; it could cross the lake almost to the mouth of the Detroit River—and there it would be stopped by the relatively shallow channels in the Detroit River, in Lake St. Clair, in the St. Clair River and in the St. Marys River. All of these were 25 feet deep in the down channel and 21 feet in the up—depths which had long been acceptable.

Moreover, on the opening of the seaway, no Great Lakes harbor had a depth of 27 feet. Three of them, Two Harbors and Presque Isle on Lake Superior and the Navy Pier by the Outer Harbor at Chicago were 26 feet deep, and three private harbors, shipping mostly ore and stone, were that same depth. But the other harbors around the lakes—more than fifty—varied from 22 to 18 feet deep.

The United States Army Corps of Engineers, North Central Division, now under General Louis J. Rumaggi, had foreseen this problem and had been making careful studies of how to solve it. Millions of dollars and years of work would be needed to change channels and harbors from depths that had been adequate for interlake shipping and for any ships that could come up the St. Lawrence River. Records showed, too, that commerce by way of even these small ships had been steadily increasing and probably would grow rapidly when the seaway was open.

Most of the channels and harbors were designed before 1920, when a lake ship 600 feet long was rare and certainly "as long as ever would be built"; a harbor 18 to 22 feet deep was thought ample.

But in 1949 a new ore boat was launched—the *Wilfred Sykes*— and suddenly every other laker looked small and old-fashioned. Since that day one of the sights at the Soo is watching this boat leave the MacArthur Lock and with a graceful turn start down the river. "There she goes!" people exclaim, and count themselves fortunate to have seen this first ship in a new era. The *Wilfred Sykes* is 678 feet long and 70 feet wide, and needs a draft of 27 feet to carry a full load, 23,000 tons. Only at the time of high water in the spring can this boat take a full cargo, but one such trip, with luck two, proved profitable. Soon other equally large boats were built. The *Wilfred Sykes* carried iron ore to steel mills at the foot of Lake Michigan; there was only the channel of the St. Marys River to consider, and that was always deepened in the spring.

After the proved success of this one ore boat, 18 large bulk freighters were added to the Great Lakes fleet and eight ocean freighters were remodeled for lake service. These 26 new carriers were 602 to 716 feet long, 67 to 75 feet wide, and needed a depth of 24.5 to 27 feet to carry full cargo of up to 25,000 tons. In 1958, two more long boats went into service, 710 and 729 feet long. Practically

Long lakers like the *Wilfred Sykes* carry iron ore from the mining country to the steel mills around the lower lakes.

the same number of crewmen can sail a larger ship, and the more powerful engines make faster voyages, allowing more trips in a season. Many of the older lake boats will be replaced by the larger ones.

In 1957, while the seaway was being constructed, the army engineers began deepening the connecting channels. They expect the work to be finished in 1962. The job is mostly dredging, though here and there dynamite crews must go ahead to break up rock ledges. Their boats make quite a colony: a large dipper-dredge, two hydraulic dredges, and a sea-going hopper-dredge. These have their own assistants: one or two tugs, a derrick-boat, a couple of launches, and several dump scows to take away the spoil. Such a fleet needs 800 to 1,000 men to operate it.

Every one of the Great Lakes channels is in constant use by ships that are pressed for time. "Get down! Unload! Hurry back!" is the aim. No captain wants to spoil his record by waiting for a dynamite crew or a fleet of dump scows. Along the busy St. Clair–Detroit River stretch, a ship passes every fifteen minutes; in one summer 30,122 craft passed a dredge crew working at full speed. And there are other problems. Sailing and motor boating are popular sports, and the region around the head of Lake Huron is a beautiful vacation area. Little boats dart around dredge fleets; the people aboard are interested and curious. The small boats dart across the route of the lakers—a captain has to be constantly alert or he will have to slow down.

Work on the channels is being done by the federal government, but improvement of harbors and building of facilities for loading, unloading, and storage must be done locally with state, urban, or private funds. Before the seaway opened, congress ordered a survey of harbors to get facts which could help toward a wise decision as to which harbors should be improved, when, and by how much work. A study such as was then undertaken had never been done and will take time, but will be very valuable. Harbor improvement is costly, and it is neither necessary nor even desirable to remake every harbor to meet the maximum depth required by a few.

Lake harbors have rather similar forms; early settlers usually chose to build their cabins by the mouth of a river. Water for drinking and cooking and the family washing was thus assured; the lake and river gave a certain mobility, too. Making a Durham boat was simple enough. Soon other settlers arrived and a village, a town, a city grew up by a river that was also a harbor. Duluth has the St. Louis River; Toledo, the Maumee; Milwaukee was especially favored with three rivers quite near each other. But there is no natural harbor on the lakes such as is found by the sea. Toronto has the nearest approach to one, being situated behind a chain of islands. As shipping increased, artificial outer harbors were made by breakwaters built in front of a city. There are several excellent outer harbors on the lake—Superior–Duluth, Milwaukee, Buffalo, and others. Other ports are shallow by seaway standards yet have good mechanical facilities for loading and unloading, for storage, and for transport. Port Arthur and Fort William on Lake Superior, in combination with railroads, ship an enormous amount of grain from western prairies; elevators at those ports can store 93,000,000 bushels of grain. Many grain boats manage the relatively shallow channels and ports; some shippers feel that even with the seaway open, it would be wise to ship to Montreal and there transship for overseas rather than discard a serviceable fleet and ship direct to Europe. Time and experience will show whether they are right.

But Cleveland with its steel mills, Milwaukee with machinery, Toledo, one of the great coal exporters, Chicago with varied products, will want to ship directly overseas as soon as feasible. For all of these cities the opening of the seaway is a challenging date.

Chicago is the only lake city that has direct water connection with the vast Mississippi basin; it has both unusual opportunity

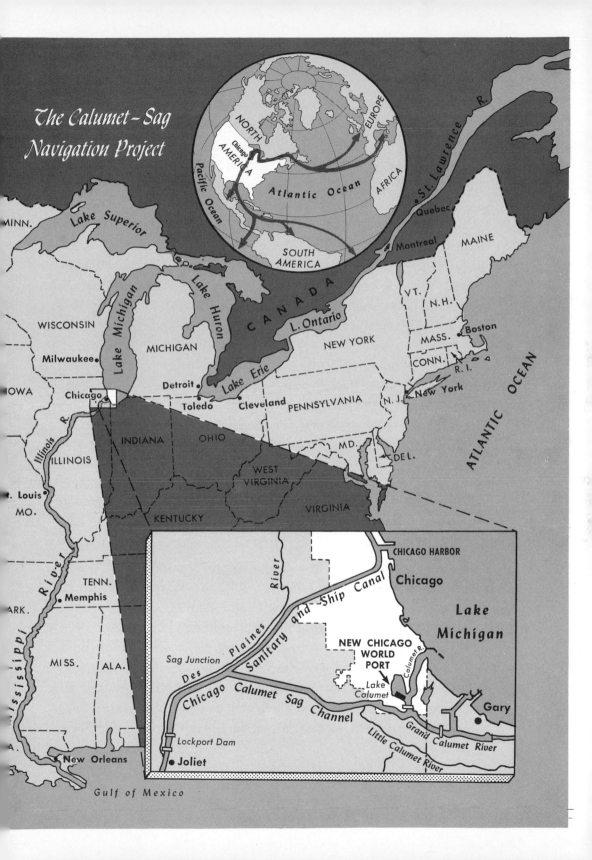

and responsibility. In the metropolitan area there are five ports: the North Branch of the Chicago River, the Chicago River near the Navy Pier and Outer Harbor, Calumet River to the south, Indiana Harbor, and Gary Harbor. The last two are in Indiana, but industrial and shipping needs make them seem a part of greater Chicago.

The Chicago River, its mouth in downtown Chicago, is the route followed by Marquette and Joliet when they went through the sag in the watershed between the Great Lakes and the Mississippi basins. The upper portion of the Illinois and Michigan Canal, opened in 1848, was replaced in 1900 as far as Lockport by the Chicago Sanitary and Ship Canal. The main purpose of this canal was to drain Chicago's scientifically treated sewage to the west instead of dumping it into the lake, from which Chicago gets its drinking water. But the new canal was made deep enough for navigation of small boats and barges.

A few years later, the state of Illinois began to canalize the Des Plaines and the Illinois rivers, but work went so slowly that the federal government, under the Rivers and Harbors Act, finished the project. The new waterway opened in 1933 as a toll-free waterway under the old Northwest Charter of 1787. In the later 1930's, the 327-mile-long waterway was further improved with better locks and dams; its 9-foot depth is ample for barges and small craft. Along this useful waterway, barges transport coal, sand, petroleum, grain, and other products which are delivered to Chicago or trans-shipped to lakers. During World War II, shipyards along Lake Michigan shores got contracts for building 1,200 war vessels—including 28 submarines—because the vessels when finished could be sent through the Illinois Waterway to the Gulf of Mexico.

The second sag, the one La Salle used when he walked to Montreal so long ago, has more recently come to public attention.

In the heart of the industrial region, along Chicago's southern shore, the Calumet River has long been a useful port. It connects with Lake Calumet, a shallow lake on a wide prairie, and with the Little Calumet River. This Little Calumet is a wanderer; it turns and makes a loop some sixteen miles from the Chicago Sanitary and Ship Canal east of Lockport, and only a little west of Chicago's city limits. In 1922 the Metropolitan Sanitary District of Greater Chicago dug a shallow channel to make the connection with the larger canal. The purpose at that time was to reverse the flow of the Little Calumet and by it, and by the small canal, drain industrial waste away from Lake Michigan. Although this Calumet Sag Channel was only sixty feet wide, it was gradually used more and more for navigation. Barges that came up the Mississippi in groups of eight or ten, pushed by a diesel tug, had to be broken up and

Barges being shoved up the Mississippi River by a towboat. Barges in a tow may carry such varied products as sugar, molasses, petroleum, edible oils, sulphur, rubber, chemicals, and steel.

taken through the little canal, one or two barges at a time. But the canal route was still cheaper than a more roundabout one. In 1956, 5,668,337 tons of cargo were moved on this narrow, shallow channel.

With all this traffic and the seaway commerce coming so soon, the army engineers began work on the channel, making it 225 feet wide and 9 feet deep, At the same time duplicate locks and other improvements are being considered for the Illinois Waterway.

Chicago's Calumet Harbor, located at the juncture of two great inland waterway systems: the Cal—Sag system, which joins the Mississippi and its tributaries, and the Great Lakes—St. Lawrence Waterway.

In addition to what the federal government is doing on the channel, the Chicago Regional Port District has built two huge, well-designed grain elevators by Lake Calumet, built long lines of modern transit sheds, and made plans for remaking Lake Calumet with slips, a channel 1,000 feet wide, and storage space for many kinds of products. There is to be special storage for edible oils— soybean oil, corn oil, and other oils, which can be transshipped to Europe. The day is very near when early dreams will be realized and Chicago will become a link between the North Atlantic Ocean and the Gulf of Mexico.

History shows that as transport is improved, the prosperity of all the people is increased. So those who are working hard on channels, harbors, and docking facilities around the lakes feel certain that such improvements will help transport more goods at less cost. No doubt much of the lake commerce will continue to be bulk shipments of grain, petroleum, iron ore, coal, and wood pulp. But cities and areas will have specialities—such as the edible oils from the Mississippi Valley—and ease and economy in moving these products will help the farmer, the shipper, the merchant, and the housewife. The economy of the United States is so interwoven that the completion of a huge project such as the seaway stirs to action many other projects; taken together these have a value far beyond what can be immediately foreseen.

CHAPTER 15

The Seaway Is Finished

THE huge plan for combined navigation and power has become a reality. Power is flowing over the wires; with the opening of the shipping season in 1959, ships used the full facilities of the seaway; the incredible dream has become a commonplace of daily navigation.

But in a sense the seaway is not "finished" and perhaps never will be. Like all improvement of the entire Great Lakes–St. Lawrence waterway, its very success will require more digging, more dredging, more construction. Already there is talk about enlarging the Welland Ship Canal or perhaps making a new arrangement of locks to separate up and down traffic all the way, not just through three twin locks. Already provision is made for more locks on the

St. Lawrence when they are needed, and no one knows how soon the province of Quebec may find need for power from the Lachine Rapids. These possibilities have been anticipated, but there will be others as larger, faster ships are built, and as commerce increases.

For three years there was some thought of using air bubbles to keep a channel ice free, a method which had proved successful in Stockholm, Sweden. Now an adaptation of this bubbling principle is used at Prescott, Ontario, actually on the seaway, to keep a channel open for a ferry. A compressor drives air bubbles up through perforations in polyethylene pipe bringing the warmer water to the surface to melt ice. Such an underwater aeration keeps a 200-foot channel entirely free of ice at 30 degrees below zero for a bridge building operation at Huntsville, Ontario. All-year-round operation is not far distant and when it comes, one of the major objections to the seaway will be removed.

During the years of discussion about the seaway, its value to adjacent states was conceded. Now the most skeptical are finding that benefits will be widely felt. Potato farmers in Maine are working on plans to build a highway through wilderness so they can get their potatoes to the port of Quebec and market them at a distance. They plan to use fishy-back trucks, modeled on the piggy-backs the railroads have found successful. Maine has wood pulp, paper, lumber, shoes, textiles, and many other articles to offer distant markets.

Benefits from the new flow of power are already felt in Ontario and in New York. New industries have brought new job opportunities. In New York, established plants are being enlarged now that there is plenty of power. Men who came from far away for temporary work are staying permanently. Many a farmer who had found it hard to make a living on a small farm can now continue to live in the country while he earns good pay at some plant not too far away. Distance means little with good cars and highways. A

1: Ships like the *Tadoussac* will carry passengers on the seaway. This scene is at Montreal. 2: A typical canaller in the Iroquois Lock, the most westerly of seven new locks built for the seaway. 3: A laker sails in the intermediate pool of the Wiley-Dondero Canal, past towers and under transmission lines from Robert Moses Power Dam. 4: A freighter of the Dutch Fjell-Oranje Lines in the St. Lawrence River immediately downstream from the Snell Lock. In the background is the U.S. army engineers' dredge *Paraiso*.

recent survey in certain areas of upper New York State showed curious changes in population; most of the people were young, under twenty, needing schools, and the very mature, over fifty. The middle, active, productive group was startlingly small. There are signs that this middle group is being attracted to the new industries that ample power is bringing. It is hoped that this attraction will continue and restore a more normal balance of population.

A pleasant surprise has been the interest the seaway inspires in other countries. Ships designed for seaway trade are on the drawing boards and in the shipyards of several countries. By the time the connecting channels are deepened, two passenger-cargo ships of the Fjell-Oranje line will be ready; these will carry 100 passengers and 9,000 tons of cargo, and will call at Rotterdam, an English port not yet announced, Montreal, and Chicago. Representatives from several European shipping lines have attended conferences and display much interest. A French travel bureau is planning a seaway cruise, like the usual Mediterranean cruise, bringing her passengers in a "floating hotel" to see the seaway attractions and visit cities on the river and the lakes.

Nor is interest confined to Europe. Japan sent delegates from an inland waterway organization and another group of industrialists. From Formosa, from Scotland, from Turkey, and other countries, groups have come to study the seaway.

Foreign shippers as well as domestic shippers were represented at the conference on toll charges in the spring of 1958. The law, according to the Wiley-Dondero Act and agreed to by Canada, requires that the loans from the United States treasury and from the Canadian government shall be paid, together with interest and maintenance charges, in fifty years. All this money must be paid from toll revenues, but it will take time and experience to determine what the toll charges should be.

Such matters are important to the business success of the seaway, but the average traveler sees beauty and mechanical perfection, not costs and commerce, as he brings his family to see the sights along the route. On a day in late summer, during one of the years of construction and dredging, vacationers stopped by the Welland Canal. On the upper level huge lakers moved with serene dignity through fragrant orchards. Down by the twin locks, long lines of automobiles were parked, their gay colors bright against the gray cement of the locks. People left cars to come close to the lock to see vessels lifted up or set down that 326 feet of the escarpment between Lake Erie and Lake Ontario. The *Scott Misener* was going up this day; the laker seemed to fill the lock completely. But no, a tug bound for Duluth slipped in to go up at the same time. Across the wall between the locks, a ship bound for Bremen, Germany, was going down; her decks were crowded with crated automobiles from Detroit.

At first the *Scott Misener* was so low in the lock that she was quite out of sight of a person sitting in a car nearby. But slowly and steadily she rose as the water, pouring quietly into the lock, bore her upward. Now the pilot house, now the deck, came level with the parkway; the crew looked pleased at the swift rise.

"Got your washing done, sailor?" a watcher called.

"I do mine Mondays," retorted the sailor. The crowd laughed; they had been held in awed silence long enough.

"Hi, Mister!" a schoolboy shouted. "How long is your boat?"

"She's 685 feet!" With a grin, the sailor added, "See how clean she is? We've just finished painting every one of those feet."

The deck was already high above the people; ahead, the big gate opened, and tug and laker moved on to the next lock. It didn't take long—15, 18 minutes a lock.

Some of the vacationers drove down to the Ontario end of the canal; they passed dry docks and other businesses related to ships. Toward the end, the road was a trail through woods, for the widened mouth of the canal is protected by long fingers of made land, well wooded, each side equipped with its own lighthouse. Entering the Welland Canal, a vessel moves slowly as though feeling its way, daunted by the great climb that is in plain sight ahead. But on leaving, it accelerates quickly, moving freely in the wide lake.

"Look! That's the *Cloverdale* again!" someone exclaimed as the name at the stern of an out-going boat came to view. "Who would have thought she'd get down from the orchards so quickly!" The laker changed her course a bit, making a mass of beautiful foam as her propeller speeded; camera enthusiasts had to hurry to get a picture before she got too far away.

"Let's stay and watch the ship for Germany come down," someone said. That ship probably carries two pilots, her own for the sea and a lake pilot. This is necessary because there is a difference between International Navigation Rules and rules that have come into usage on the lakes. For instance, ocean ships blow one blast at not more than two-minute intervals for fog, while lake rules require three short blasts every minute. Those three short blasts at sea mean, "My engine is going full speed astern." No particular signal indicates danger at sea, but on the lakes several short, rapid blasts mean trouble. Rules for lights are different, too.

In time, if ocean-going ships use the seaway, as now seems probable, pilots will come to know both sets of rules. Or, better still, there will be changes to make signals uniform.

Crossing Lake Ontario, a ship going east will travel through the deepened Thousand-Island section, through the Iroquois Lock, and into the new Lake St. Lawrence. The engineers who planned the vast changes in the landscape in the international section of the seaway provided new beauty as they destroyed the old. The huge boulders and the tossing white foam of centuries are gone, but in their place quiet waters of the long new lake lap wooded shores. The music of the waters, the songs of the *coureurs de bois* are gone,

Montreal's harbor on the St. Lawrence River makes it one of the most important seaports of North America. The river front and the harbor stretch for about sixteen miles along the north bank of the St. Lawrence.

but now groups of vacationers sing around campfires, and radios bring music from distant cities. Sailboats, speedboats, and outboards have neat berths near the camps, and day and night great liners and lakers move by on the river.

As a ship enters the seaway opposite Montreal, passengers will see high above that busy port the mountain Jacques Cartier climbed. By the wharfs below the city is the spot where Samuel de Champlain landed and talked with the Indians; not far away is the site of La Salle's farm. These men of daring wanted to find the riches of Cathay.

Today, men of vision have brought to completion their search for riches of a very practical sort—at home. As the long years of discussion end with success, the world can see that when countries work with one another, as have the United States of America and the Dominion of Canada in the creation of the seaway, further miracles are also possible, miracles as great as men's dreams.